1st Book of Devotionals

John "Cleve" Stafford

Published by John "Cleve" Stafford, 2024.

1ST BOOK OF DEVOTIONALS

Second edition. February 15, 2024.

Copyright © 2024 John "Cleve" Stafford.

ISBN: 979-8-9900544-1-7

Written by John "Cleve" Stafford.

Table of Contents

Chapter 1
Blueprint for Life

God, the Creator of heaven and earth (**Gen. 1:1**), sent His beloved Son (**Mat. 3:17**) through whom all things were made (**Joh. 1:3**) into the world when the time was right (**Gal. 4:4**) to manifest a new truth through Him (**Heb. 1:2**). This truth we would receive from the Word (**Rom. 10:17**), which is the very utterances of God (**1Pe. 4:11**), who cannot lie (**Tit. 1:2**). God did that because He loved us (**1Jo. 4:19**), whom He knew in our mother's womb (**Jer. 1:5; Psa. 139:13**). He would give his only Son (**Joh. 3:16**), who was with Him at the beginning of time (**Gen. 1:26; Joh. 1:1**), while we were yet sinners (**Rom. 5:8**) and worthy of death (**Rom. 6:23**), to die for us. Jesus did this by becoming the propitiation for our sins (**Rom. 3:25**), suffering and dying on a cross, and bearing our sins for us so that we may live in righteousness (**1Pe. 2:24**).

In turn, it allowed us to be justified through faith in Christ (**Gal. 2:16**) as a gift (**Rom. 3:24**). Because of that, have the hope to live eternally (**Rom. 6:23**) in heaven, a place of such beauty that it defies understanding (**1Co. 2:9**). To receive the blessing of His work on the cross, we need to hear the word (**Rom. 10:17**), believe it to be so (**Mar. 16:19; Rom. 10:14**), repent of our sins (**Act. 3:19**), and confess that Christ, our Lord, and Savior, is the Son of the One True God and Creator, (**Rom. 10:9-10**), truly knowing that He is the way, the truth and the life (**Joh. 14:6-7**) and that there is salvation in no other name under heaven (**Act. 4:12**), and then be buried with Him in Baptism (**Col. 2:12; Rom. 6:4**) in the name of the Father, Son, and Holy Spirit (**Mat. 28:19**), not by sprinkling, but by immersion (**Act. 8:38**) in order to receive remission of our sins and the gift of the Holy Spirit (**Act. 2:38-9**), who will then dwell in us (**2Ti. 1:14; Rom. 8:9**) and intercede for us (**Rom. 8:26**), as Christ Himself does (**Rom. 8:34**).

From that day on, we should strive to obey (**Rom. 6:17**), putting away all bitterness, wrath, anger, clamor, slander, and malice (**Eph. 4:31**), knowing that we were saved by His grace and not by anything we did or could do (**Eph. 2:8-9**), admitting that we will falter at times (**1Jo. 1:8**) but will receive His forgiveness (**1Jo. 1:9**) if we repent (**Act. 8:22**), but also understanding that to receive that forgiveness, we too need to forgive as well. (**Col. 3:13; Mat. 6:14-15**), and never return evil for evil (**Rom. 12:17**), loving God with all of our heart, soul, and mind (**Mat. 22:37**), and our neighbors as ourselves (**Mar. 12:31**) while thanking him for our blessings (**Eph. 5:20; 1Th. 5:18**).

In doing so, we should go to church and encourage one another (**Heb. 10:25**), sing psalms and hymns (**Eph. 5:19; Col. 3:16**), and remember our Savior by partaking in Communion (**Luk. 22:19-20**) once weekly (**Act. 20:7**). As men, we need to be dignified, respectful, and temperate (**Tit. 2:2**) and love our wives as Christ Himself loved the church (**Eph. 5:25**). And women should submit to their husbands, as to the Lord (**Eph. 5:22**). We should not provoke our children but discipline and instruct them in the Lord (**Col. 3:21, Eph. 6:4**) so that they do not depart from the word (**Pro. 22:6**). Children of all ages should love and respect their parents (**Mat. 19:19**) as we are commanded to do (**Eph. 6:2-3**).

We should be examples to the people in the world, and our light should shine before us to bring glory to our Father in heaven (**Mat. 5:16**), and we should make disciples of all nations and teach them the things concerning God (**Mat. 28:20**). We should strive to be like Christ at all times (**ICo. 11:1; Eph. 5:1-2**), knowing that if we do so to the end of our lives if we run the race with endurance that is set before us (**Heb. 12:1**), we will be judged accordingly (**Act. 17:31; Rom. 2:6**) and receive the crown of life (**Jam. 1:12; 2Ti. 4:8**), and a room in that mansion (**Joh. 14:2**).

All this can only be achieved, however, if Christ is our cornerstone (**Eph. 2:20**), we meditate on the Word day and night (**Jos. 1:8**), and we learn to pray for what we want unceasingly (**ITh. 5:17**), knowing that we will receive it (**Mar. 11:24**), believing that all things work together for the good of those who love the Lord (**Rom. 8:28**), and then putting our belief into action (**Jam. 1:22**) and cultivate the fruit of the spirit – love, joy, peace, patience, kindness, goodness, faithfulness, gentleness and self-control (**Gal. 5:22-23**), all the while crucifying flesh with all its passions and desires (**Gal. 5:24**). Now, tell me the Bible is not a blueprint for life.

Chapter 2

You Are the Most Beautiful Person in the World

"For You formed my inward parts; You knitted me together in my mother's womb" (**Psa. 139:13**). During my time as a youth minister, more than one teen came to me for help with self-image problems. I recall one particularly distressing conversation when a beautiful young girl sat in my office. As often would happen, one of the teens would come and visit with me just for the sake of doing so. We would discuss their families, school, a crush, youth ministry, or whatever else they wished to discuss. It was during one of those treasured, unannounced visits that she suddenly blurted out, "People think I am ugly!"

I remember being shocked as she uttered those words, and I will never forget the look of sadness on her face. It was evident that this issue was causing her a great deal of pain. She was not unpopular and had many friends, so it was surprising that she thought people viewed her as ugly. As I looked at her sad face, trying to decide the best way to respond, I realized something; "There has never been an ugly woman, just a man with bad taste." For someone to even consider a creation of God ugly is to say that He made a mistake. We all know God does not make mistakes, so why do we think one person is ugly while another is beautiful?

The young, perturbed teen sitting in my office was certainly not ugly, but she was making the mistake we all so often do. She was viewing herself through the lens of society instead of God. We are conditioned to label someone "beautiful" or "ugly" from a very young age. Hollywood, television, and other forms of media like books and magazines all play their part in developing our misguided views of what constitutes the "perfect" man or woman. When we meet someone beautiful, we sometimes hear, "Wait until the first morning when she has no makeup on...lol." Few people doubt that makeup smooths out the blemishes we think we have, and nothing is wrong with that.

But often, it is taken to the extreme, with liberal amounts being used to try and fit Hollywood's picture of health and beauty. With the advent of "filters," we can use apps to transform ourselves to look like someone society deems perfect. I powered up my computer and searched "Movie stars without makeup." Together, we looked at the images of one star after another who was brave enough to be seen without makeup. "They don't look the same as we see them in magazines and movies, but they still are beautiful, aren't they?" I asked. She agreed.

You see, most people laugh at those "untouched" pictures because they fail to see the natural beauty of God's creations. Who cares what all the world thinks? Allow yourself to see your God-given beauty and find your happiness in that person. Don't try to be beautiful for the world and seek its adoration; be beautiful for yourself, and someone out there will find you "gorgeous." When He formed you, He also formed someone who will think you are the most beautiful person in the world.

Chapter 3
There Are Too Many Fools

"A fool says in his heart, 'There is no God.' They are corrupt, they do abominable deeds" (**Psa. 14:1**). Most of us know this verse, even if it is only the first part. There are many reasons people choose not to believe in God, but whatever the reason, it is sad when they do. We make a conscious decision to accept or reject the idea of God. Either we confess we are sinners in need of salvation and embrace the redemptive work of Christ, or we don't care to admit our sin(s), and we say, "He does not exist." For the latter group, the total rejection of God stems from a variety of reasons, but it almost always relates to the second part of the verse, "They are corrupt, they do abominable deeds." Believing in God requires something they are not prepared to do – repent.

They enjoy their licentious lifestyles, vile manners, crude language, and hateful, arrogant attitudes, so their only option is to reject God and His commandments altogether. To admit there is a God means they would have to confront their sinful nature, and that burden is too heavy for them to bear. It is far easier to convince themselves that there is no God because they can shirk the responsibility of living a Christian lifestyle. They do not want to be accountable for their actions, so they call believers "stupid," "delusional," and "Idiots" and falsely believe their faulty moral compass is functioning correctly.

Once they think that, they are absolved from any wrongdoing in their mind because they "know" what is right and wrong. Sin, if they even consider what they are doing as such, has no consequence in their fantasy world, and they can revel in their debauchery and depravity. So, instead of falling to their knees in contrite repentance and accepting forgiveness from the Almighty, they convince themselves He does not exist – to their eternal doom. The willful rejection and replacement of God by themselves will cost them dearly. Their present lifestyle, as pleasurable and free from accountability as it may seem, will result in a torturous prison of fire for eternity.

If only they knew how impossible it is to hide their sin from God and how easy it is to be forgiven. Maybe then they would make a better choice. God does not wish anyone to die in sin, "...not wishing that any should perish, but that all should reach repentance." (**2Pe. 3:9**). He is patient as He waits for them to come to their senses. But they should not be fooled into thinking that He will not repay them for their transgressions if He does exist. God is loving, graceful, merciful, and kind, but He will not be mocked, and a price will be exacted for rejecting Him. If you know someone like that, pray for them.

Pray they will come to their senses and depart from their evil ways before it is too late. Pray fervently that they will reach out and embrace the light that is their salvation. But above all, be an example of what God expects of them. Show them by your words and actions the freedom we live in and the joy we have, knowing that the glory of heaven awaits us. Maybe then they will want what we have.

Chapter 4

Fight to Save One More Person

"I want you to know, brothers, that what has happened to me has really served to advance the Gospel so that it has become known throughout the whole imperial guard and to all the rest that my imprisonment is for Christ. And most of the brothers, having become confident in the Lord by my imprisonment, are much more bold to speak the word without fear" (**Php. 1:12-14**).

Not everyone is as fortunate as you are on this beautiful day with which the Lord has blessed us. Some are in danger every moment as they courageously take the Gospel to areas in dire need of it. Their safety is not guaranteed, but their loyalty to God is such that they are willing to suffer persecution and even death to spread the Good News.

We should be thankful for these brave warriors of God's word and support them in any way we can. They do not allow their situation to defeat their mission, and neither should we. Your life may not be at risk, but you may still find yourself in some degree of persecution, and if you do, Paul wants you to know something. You are not alone. Some brothers and sisters are going through the same and even worse, and their courage should inspire you to be bolder, just as Paul's situation emboldened those in his day. Few of us face physical danger because of our religion, and fewer still do so under the threat of death, so why do we hesitate to spread the Good News?

What are we so afraid of? Is it the opinion of mankind that prevents us from uttering "Jesus loves you" to someone who may be desperately seeking guidance and comfort? If that is the case, take courage from the words of **Mat. 10:28**, "And do not fear those who kill the body but cannot kill the soul. Rather fear Him who can destroy both soul and body in hell." Do not take it as a threat but rather as an indication of the power of God. Whose side would you rather be on, mortal man with his limited capacity to harm you, or God who has your entire "forever" in His hands? Stop having an earthly fear of man and instead have a spiritual fear of God.

Furthermore, you are not alone in the struggles you face in your daily life. We have much to learn from other Christians; their similar problems can be a great source of encouragement if we allow it to be. Take to heart the words of 1Pe. 5:8-9,

> "Be sober-minded; be watchful. Your adversary the devil prowls around like a roaring lion, seeking someone to devour. Resist him, firm in your faith, knowing that the same kinds of suffering are being experienced by your brotherhood throughout the world."

There is comfort in knowing that we are not alone in the persecutions we face.

Was He not considered an outcast, an upstart who would be here today and gone tomorrow? And yet He was willing to go to that cross to suffer humiliation and death to give you the underserved opportunity of salvation. Fight to save one more person. Fight to give someone the same opportunity that was given to you. Help them to a better future and don't be afraid. You are not alone. "...for He has said, "I will never leave you nor forsake you." (**Heb. 13:5**).

Chapter 5
An Ode to Mothers

"Strength and dignity are her clothing, and she laughs at the time to come. She opens her mouth with wisdom, and the teaching of kindness is on her tongue. She looks well to the ways of her household and does not eat the bread of idleness. Her children rise and call her blessed; her husband also, and he praises her: 'Many women have done excellently, but you surpass them all" (**Pro. 31:25-30**).

Today, I want to look at a very special person in our lives. All of them sacrificed considerably, but some even gave their lives to ensure our birth. For months they were uncomfortable because of the loss of mobility to one degree or another.

Their bodies nourished us, kept us warm, and provided us with a place of safety and security. They soothed us with song and gentle touches as they stroked their extended bellies in acts of pure love for the tiny life within its confines. Theirs were the first words we heard. As we took our first breath, we cried – until we were placed into their arms and heard that familiar voice, soothing us with words of love and encouragement. They fed us, stayed up night after night to comfort us, provided for us, clothed us, and continued to protect us with courage that is hard to imagine.

They showed us off to the world, introduced us to solid food, taught us to say our first word, and protected us like a mama bear her cub. They cared for us, crying in anguish when we were sick, and yet never showed us their pain. Instead, they whispered prayers to God and promised in our ears that everything would be okay. We heard those whispers and instinctively knew all would be well. They watched us play and played with us even when they had so many other things to do because we were never a distraction to them.

They took our hands and showed us how to shape the letters of our names and draw "pictures" of the family. Their hearts broke as they dropped us off for our first day of school, even though they bravely said, "Enjoy, my baby. You will meet new friends and learn all the things of the world here." They cried as they watched us run off with our friends, but all we saw when we turned back was a smile and a wave. They took us to church for the first time, sang "Jesus loves me," and recited "Now I lay me down to sleep..." every night until the words were ingrained in our memories.

They watched us grow from infants to toddlers, to teens and beyond. They were beautiful and brilliant, always had the correct answer, and were the one place we would return to when sick or hurting. We did not know when they were ill as they soldiered on, bravely hiding their pain so as not to worry us. Through our tumultuous teen years, they were there, guiding us, praying that we would not stray from the path of righteousness, and if we did, they prayed even more fervently that we would find our way back.

When we left with friends for our first camp or date, we did not see the tears. All we saw when we looked back was that familiar smile and wave we had seen so many times before. They would go out and work or stay at home and work all day. They would prepare our food, help us with our homework, and clean the house. They would bathe and prepare us for bed. Then, when we were sleeping soundly, they would go and do the ironing and prepare our food for the next day at school. They would do this daily without complaint, treasuring us in a way we would not appreciate for decades.

They were always brave, always honest, always loyal, always trustworthy. They remained at our side even when we became aggressive and recalcitrant as young adults trying to find our place in the world. Even if we abused them with disparaging words, mocked them, or ignored them, they remained at our side. We stormed out of the house angry because we could not or would not understand their reasoning. We did not realize the heartbreak our actions caused, brushing them off with disdain at times. Their love knew no bounds; it still does not.

They looked at us with pride even though we failed occasionally because, for them, nothing we ever did was a failure, just a learning experience. Every kiss was a band-aid that "made it better," and every warm smile, loving hug, and word of encouragement etched themselves into our hearts forever, even if we did not realize it then. They were not afraid to punish us when needed, but let a stranger touch us, and the mama bear would come out with unequaled ferocity.

As our dating years began, they were there to share in the joy of our "first love" and were there when it ended to lend us a shoulder to cry on. One day they would watch us walk down the aisle as we began to forge our own families, and when we looked back, we saw it again – the familiar wave and encouraging smile. Tears still accompanied it, but those tears represented joy and hope this time. Even if that hope were to be shattered by divorce one day, they would still welcome us home, and we would once again have that shoulder to cry on.

And no matter our age, until their dying day, we will always be their "baby." Think of that as you open your presents on your birthday or December 25th while she catches the wrapping paper. Enjoy all your gifts but remember the best one of all. Think of what she has done as she prepares the food, and you play with your gifts. Think of all she has done as you snooze after an "exhausting" morning while she is washing the dishes and picking up your mess. Think of all she has done as you glance at her, older now and gray, but still giving you that wave and that smile. Look closely; she is just as beautiful, just as smart, just as dedicated, and just as loyal as she ever was – the embodiment of all that is good in your world.

Think of all she has done as she showers your children with the same love you had showered on you. And be thankful that you have a great mother who was a great teacher. Maybe tell her how much you love her. Maybe hug her and tell her how much she means to you. Maybe tell her that all your good parts are the parts she shared with you. Maybe tell her she is the best mother you could ever have wished for. You know what, forget "maybe" – go and do it while you still can.

Chapter 6

Whom Do You Serve?

"Now, therefore, fear the Lord and serve him in sincerity and in faithfulness. Put away the gods that your fathers served beyond the River and in Egypt, and serve the Lord. And if it is evil in your eyes to serve the Lord, choose this day whom you will serve, whether the gods your fathers served in the region beyond the River or the gods of the Amorites in whose land you dwell. But as for me and my house, we will serve the Lord" (**Jos. 24:14-15**).

Most of us have a plaque, or something similar with this verse inscribed on it, put up somewhere in our house.

But I wonder how many people take the time to truly understand what is being stated, and, if they do, how much energy they invest in following it. Talk is cheap, but following that up with actions is costly. It takes courage and commitment to follow God in a world that rejects His commands and rejects Him. Moreover, saying that you serve the Lord is entirely different from actually doing so. **Rom. 1:16** states, "I am not ashamed of the Gospel..." but sadly, that is precisely what millions of Christians worldwide are.

They serve the Lord while in church or around Christian friends but put Him in a small container at the bottom of a drawer somewhere for the rest of the week. Until they return to church or the company of Christian friends, they serve the world and all its idols instead. They desire the fleeting admiration and accolades of the world so much that they do anything within their power to be "one of them." Then, when it is time again, they search for the little container, put it in their pocket, and pretend to be "all about God and His business." Even if they profess to be a Christian all the time, their actions belie their empty words.

They may fool others and even themselves, but they will do well to remember that they do not fool God. Their lifestyle makes a mockery of their so-called Christian faith, and in doing so, mocks God – but **Gal. 6:7** should serve as a dire warning to these individuals, "Do not be deceived: God will not be mocked...". All our actions have consequences, and the all-seeing eye of our Lord God sees absolutely everything we do. Here is one more scripture they should heed: "Not everyone who says to me, Lord, Lord, will enter the kingdom of heaven..." (**Mat. 7:21**).

You will need more than lip service to earn a room in that mansion. Pretending to serve God while serving the world is a recipe for disaster that will have everlasting repercussions. Do you really want to be on the wrong side of eternity that day we are all called to answer for our deeds on earth? So, next time you read that sign, pause for self-reflection for a moment and consider whom you serve – your choice has eternal consequences.

Chapter 7

When the Happiest Time of the Year Isn't

"...I will never leave you nor forsake you" (**Heb. 13:5**). If you believe the Bible and honestly believe it is the inspired Word breathed out by the Almighty God, this is one of the most comforting verses. I think we can all agree that there are times when the future looks particularly bleak. Times when your finances are not doing so well, you lose a job you need, your marriage has run onto some rocky ground, a friendship you cherished suddenly ended, or someone you love gets taken from this life.

The joy we are supposed to feel at the happiest time of the year is stolen from us, and we are left with nothing but despair. You may throw your hands in the air at times like that and exclaim, "Why?" If you are suffering one or more of those kinds of difficulties, I want to tell you that millions of us are praying for a solution for your pain to ease. We may not know your name or where you live, but in our prayers, we always ask God to comfort those dealing with tragedies.

I know you feel abandoned by God. You may be angry and have questioned His very existence, but I am here to tell you, "God has not abandoned you." When your strength and resolve have left you, lean on Him to restore you. Read the words of scripture we started and ended with this morning often and let them sink in. Remember the stories of the characters in the Bible who thought God had abandoned them only to realize there was something much better ahead for them.

I am not minimizing your grief if you have lost someone; I, too, will spend this Christmas without a cherished one, but I believe that God took him as part of a plan beyond my understanding. On the way home from picking up my son and daughter from the airport, she received a call from her boss to say the company had experienced a financial disaster and they were all being let go. If you are dealing with one, two, or even more tragedies, please do not lose faith in Him. Rightfully grieve because it is part of the healing process, but don't let grief or anger remove you from the presence of God.

Try to understand that there is a much bigger plan than we can fathom. Thank God for the lessons learned, the time we were fortunate to spend with someone, and His embrace of your loved one who is no longer hurting. Trust God to open new opportunities and give you the courage and wisdom to restore damaged relationships. Moreover, trust Him to bear your burden of agonizing loss with you until you can smile again.

Allow God to grow you through those trials and increase your faith as a result. I cannot always answer the "Why?" No one can, but we can tell you that nothing happens outside the will of God, even when it seems to have.

> "For My thoughts are not your thoughts, neither are your ways My ways' declares the Lord. 'As the heavens are higher than the earth, so are My ways higher than your ways and My thoughts than your thoughts." (**Isa. 55:8-9**).

Chapter 8
Confusing Words

Several words in the Bible are not that easy to understand. Among them are the following: atonement, propitiation, redemption, justified, righteous, and sanctified. On more than one occasion, an individual has asked me to explain them. Usually, I define each term and then use them in a sentence to clarify their meaning.

Christ was the atonement for the sins of everyone, thereby becoming the propitiation and ensuring the believer's redemption to be justified as righteous and then be sanctified.

Atonement is universal in nature and refers to Christ's death for every person. It was the reconciliation of God and humanity through Christ's work on the cross. It allows any individual who desires to approach God to do so with the secure knowledge that they will not be rejected despite their sinful nature.

Propitiation refers to Christ's work in appeasing or satisfying God, whose anger was kindled against humanity's sins. The atonement paved the way for alleviating God's righteous anger toward His people because of their constant sinful actions.

Redemption is personal in nature and is the blood spilled on the cross for the individual believer. Whereas atonement and propitiation happened at a specific point in the past, redemption began with the blood of Christ but flowed forward to affect the seeker at Baptism. In essence, it delivers them from sin to enable the following action by God.

Justification refers to God's act of moving an individual from a state of injustice, which is sin, to one of justice, which is grace and mercy. It is an acquittal, similar to a judge declaring someone free from the accusation of a crime in court.

Righteous refers to the state of right standing before Him because He justified us. It is ongoing by nature, dependent on our obedience, of course.

Sanctification means being set apart from the rest of the world. It gives us the strength to grow in our spirituality.

I usually use the following sentence to illustrate their relationship: "Christ was the atonement for the sins of everyone, thereby becoming the propitiation and ensuring the believer's redemption, to be justified as righteous and sanctified."

Chapter 9
Faith Like That is Power

Have you ever prayed for something and felt like God did not answer you? At times like that, you may feel like the writer of **Psa. 22:1-2**,

> "My God, my God, why have you forsaken me? Why are you so far from saving me, from the words of my groaning? O my God, I cry by day, but you do not answer, and by night, but I find no rest."

Many times, you have prayed with the wrong motivation. We pray for entirely the wrong reasons and then cannot understand why God is "ignoring" us. In **Jam. 4:3**, the writer tells us the following, "You ask and do not receive, because you ask wrongly, to spend it on your passions."

When we ask God to win the lottery to buy a bigger house or drive a fancier car, God hears the prayer but does not respond. We may even try to convince Him of all the good we will do with the money once we win it, but He knows our hidden motivations, even if we try to hide them deep within us. But what of the times we approach His throne on our proverbial knees and beg for something worthwhile? Those prayers are not self-seeking; they are not even about us. They are genuine, fervent, and desperate. They are not even for our well-being but for that of another person. The individual may be gravely ill.

Their situation is dire, and we are driven to our knees in prayer. We pray continuously with all our might, but our prayers are unanswered. Instead of overcoming the illness, they succumb to it and pass on from this life. Our prayers for that person did not come from a place of selfish motivation but a genuine concern for them, so why did God not answer our prayers – why did we get a hard "no"? The harsh reality is that for most of the time, no one on earth will be able to give you a satisfactory answer that will remove your grief and disappointment at the outcome.

But there is a scripture that answers it for us. I am, of course, speaking of **Isa. 55:8-9**

"For My thoughts are not your thoughts, neither are your ways My ways, declares the Lord. For as the heavens are higher than the earth, so are My ways higher than your ways and My thoughts than your thoughts."

Will this magically take away your pain? No, but faith will help you understand that some things are beyond our understanding. At times like that, we must rely on our steadfast faith, knowing that God has a reason, and there will come a time when that reason will be available to us.

True faith trusts God more than our understanding of events. It is predicated on the belief that God is the Alpha and Omega, and everything happens within His will. Faith like that is power – the power to understand and overcome any difficulty.

Chapter 10
Admire Versus Desire

"He who finds a wife finds a good thing and obtains favor from the Lord" (**Pro. 18:22**). Men, do you realize what you have in your chosen wife? Too many men find themselves gazing with desire at other women as their marriage becomes "stale." They have enjoyed their wife so many times that she loses the "luster" he initially perceived in her. Before long, he begins searching for a newer, shinier trophy to conquer and display for all the world to see.

When he finds her, he "dumps" the "love of his life," as he so often called her, and makes off with the other woman. Too often, there are also children who must suffer the consequences of his roving eye. But his desire to touch something new, feel like a teenager again, and enjoy the pleasures of new "flesh" overshadows the need to be a faithful husband and good role model for his children. I do not believe it's wrong to admire the beauty of another human being. My wife and I can appreciate another man's or woman's personal attributes, but we distinguish between "admire and desire."

Admiring someone does not have the same characteristics desire has attached to it. Admiring someone does not always include only their outward appearance. More often than not, it is based on an appreciation of their grace, poise, love for other people, and a host of other excellent properties they display daily. That is not the case with desire, however. It is not an observation but a selfish emotion that wants to conquer the object of desire. It craves with no regard to the pain conquering him/her will inflict on others.

Everything that was once good is left behind in pursuit of the new. Let's take a look at what is being left behind. A woman you treasured enough to commit to but whom you now consider waste; one you would gladly have fought a wild animal to protect but now treat worse than one. A woman whom you proudly called "love," "baby," "wifey," or some other unique name but now call the worst of names. You honored her with the promise of your loyalty and dedication but now dishonor her with defilement.

What is left behind is someone who admired you even as your body began to lose its youthful appearance. She carried you on a pedestal and treated you like a king, even when you acted like a clown. She cared for you when you acted like a baby every time you became ill, and she gladly suffered the ravages of childbirth to provide you with children. She was there at your side during your best and worst moments in life. She laughed at your silly jokes because she actually thought you were funny, even though you probably were not.

She never desired another man over you and could not imagine life without you. Her best years have been yours to enjoy. When she adoringly spoke your name, others admired her loyalty to you. She did not care what others thought of you and defended you without hesitation. Stop looking at what you don't have and look at what is yours before it is too late. Stop desiring before what is said of this remarkable woman you don't deserve is said in past tense.

Chapter 11

Your Spiritual Fire Extinguisher, Repentance

"Can a man carry fire next to his chest and his clothes not be burned? Or can one walk on hot coals and his feet not be scorched?" (**Pro. 6:27-28**). These are two of the lesser-known verses in the Bible, but ones that bear a message well worth learning. Most of the world, including many Christians, carry worldliness close to their hearts. Saying that you are carrying something next to your chest is illustrative of somehow trying to protect it or that it is near and dear to you. Often, man has sin so dear to him that he carries it near his heart. The problem is that not only can our clothes be burned, but we can also be.

Let me explain it to you using a personal example when I was a young, 25-year-old man. My dad and I owned a trucking company, and I was cleaning truck parts in gasoline. At the time, I was a cigarette smoker. At some point during the morning, I wanted to do what so many smokers do several times during the day – take a break for a "smoke." I withdrew my hands from the container and started walking away from it. I knew the dangers of a naked flame near fuel, so I wanted to enjoy the cigarette a distance away, but habit is a hard thing to break. I had barely turned when I placed a cigarette in my mouth and struck a match.

The open flame did not set the large container with the fuel in it on fire, but it did catch the residual gasoline on my hand on fire. I immediately panicked and instinctively hit that hand with the other one. Of course, that did not extinguish the flame but rather caused my other hand to catch fire as well. Thankfully, I saw an extinguisher near me and put out the flame, but I will never forget the fear I felt in those few seconds. The habit I had kept close to my chest could have caused me great pain and may even have cost me my life that fateful day. I eventually quit smoking.

The second verse refers to someone scorching their feet by walking on hot coals. Some people intentionally walk across hot coals for a tradition or even for fun, but none of them can linger too long before being burned. Others may accidentally stumble onto hot coals because they are not paying attention, much like the time I set myself on fire. When we walk in the world and all its sins, intentionally or because we are not vigilant to the dangers around us, we will be burned. It is impossible to walk on the coals of worldliness and not scorch your feet. It is far safer to remove that habit from your life, thus eliminating the chances of being hurt.

If you find yourself on fire, figuratively speaking, reach for the spiritual extinguisher, repentance, and put out the flames before you are permanently scarred or lose your life.

Chapter 12
Feeding Ourselves

"Now these Jews were more noble than those in Thessalonica; they received the Word with all eagerness, examining the scriptures daily to see if these things were so" (**Act. 17:11**).

Many years ago, city authorities were alerted to an extraordinary and tragic event happening to some pelicans on their beaches in San Diego, California. For some unknown reason, pelicans were starving to death by the hundreds. Wildlife authorities and researchers alike were dumbfounded by the deaths for a while.

Food contamination was initially suspected, but soon, it was disproved, and sicknesses and various other ideas were investigated. Eventually, it was discovered that man's benevolence was destroying these beautiful creatures. For years, the pelicans were the benefactors of discarded waste from the fishing industry. When throwing fish waste into the bay was stopped, the tragedy unfolded. Since food was so readily available, the art of fishing was not passed on to their young anymore.

As a result, they could not provide for themselves, and they ended up starving to death. Alaskan pelicans were introduced into the area in a rather creative solution, and fishing practices soon returned to normal. Spiritually speaking, we can be just like those pelicans. Our biblical diet can be so spoon-fed to us that we lose the ability to "search the scriptures" for ourselves. The result is that we starve spiritually. We cannot rely solely on those teaching and preaching to feed us – it is up to us to learn to feed ourselves.

Moreover, we need to learn the art of self-feeding to know what we are being fed. We may inadvertently, or worse, purposely be poisoned with false teachings. If we cannot discern false doctrines, we will end up dying in an unsaved state. Many people are too lazy or simply don't care what they are being fed. They go to church, ingest whatever is thrown before them, and then leave, ticking the "Gone to church" box. Why would we leave such a critical thing as our eternal salvation in the hands of another? We may not have the gift to teach or preach, but we all can study for ourselves.

While the importance of sound teachers and preachers cannot be overstated, we must take responsibility for our spiritual growth. We can only accomplish that by studying and meditating on the Word of God. That is the only sure way to mature as Christians and strive to be more Christlike in our behavior. So, accept the spiritual food with a measure of thankfulness and then go home and meditate on it. Preachers and teachers are not perfect either. They may inadvertently be teaching something incorrectly, and careful study could help them see and correct the mistake.

We are all students of the Word, irrespective of age, spiritual maturity, education, or standing in the church. Don't wait; start learning the art of feeding yourself today.

Chapter 13
The Signs Are Always There

"For I know the plans I have for you, declares the Lord, plans for welfare and not for evil, to give you a future and a hope" (**Jer. 29:11**). I absolutely believe God has a plan for our lives. Sometimes, it is evident; sometimes, it is a little less clear; other times, we only see it with the wisdom of hindsight. One thing is sure, though: He always has our best interests at heart. The example I like to use to illustrate my point is driving a vehicle. At times, the weather is clear. It is a beautiful summer day, and the sun is shining brightly.

All the road signs are clear, and we can follow their directions easily. They will significantly help us reach our destination in the most timely and efficient manner. At other times, it is like driving in the dark. We must slow down and pay more attention since we cannot see as clearly as in the daytime. The signs might be less readily visible, but if we look carefully, we will see them and still reach our destination, albeit a little slower. Yet other times, it rains, and driving becomes more hazardous.

As the rain pelts down around us, we must pay meticulous attention to our surroundings lest we miss the signs. That requires us to drive even more slowly. Then there are times, in dense fog when the signs are there, but the weather has made it almost impossible to see, and we must be cautious not to miss them. It is not that they have disappeared or fallen over, but they are practically invisible, even at short distances. The most dangerous of all is when there is ice on the road.

The dangers of driving can distract us from our route and make us lose our way. During more difficult times, speed is the enemy of our progress and can result in us never reaching our destination. The last example is when we choose to go our own way, disregarding the signs and just "wing it." We are convinced we know the way and stumble along, using only our "good sense of direction." Of course, at times, our "good sense" is severely lacking, and we end up lost.

Slow down and look for the signs...they are there even if they don't always appear to be. And, whatever you do, stay on the road...don't try to take a shortcut without precisely knowing if it will allow you to reach your destination promptly. Don't wing it through life. You have the Bible, and you have prayer – use it.

Chapter 14

Is It a Betrayal?

"For I am not ashamed of the gospel, for it is the power of God for salvation to everyone who believes, to the Jew first and also to the Greek" (**Rom. 1:16**). Paul says he is not ashamed of the gospel and then proceeds to qualify his statement with the fact that it has the power to save everyone. But it is the first eight words I want to concentrate on this morning, "For I am not ashamed of the gospel...." As a minister, I have witnessed far too many people who cannot claim the same as Paul. They are the proverbial "saint" when they are within the confines of the church building and attend all the functions faithfully.

People look at them, sometimes with astonishment, because of the perceived level of loyalty to Christ, but no sooner do they exit the building than they hide their "Christianity." These people only touch a Bible for something related to the church but never glance at it during other times. They return to work and act like the world. They tell and laugh at crude jokes, make fun of others, and act in ways contrary to God's Word. They trade their fake obedience to the Word for the fleeting enjoyment of the world and all its sins.

Ask them if they are a Christian in church, and they will laugh at you. "Of course we are!" they will reply – astonished that you would ask them such an insulting question. And by all accounts, at least in the context and vicinity of the auditorium, they are, but meet them in the week at their place of business, and they will portray an entirely different picture. They wear their Christianity on their sleeve like a tattoo, proudly displaying their beliefs among brothers and sisters in Christ. Then, when they leave, they wipe off the tattoo so that it does not betray their weekly persona.

You see, that tattoo is not permanent, but rather a temporary one that can be removed quickly when they are among their "other" friends. They will excuse their behavior by saying things like, "But Paul became everything to everyone" or "I am only doing that to slip in under the radar and then invite them to church." But the world does not see a Christian with a plan. It sees an individual who is ashamed of the gospel, ashamed to admit who they are and what they stand for, hiding their God for fear of being mocked or persecuted by the world.

If you do that, if you act like Christ is your Lord on Sunday but are ashamed to admit that during the week, then you need to be really careful.

Your end will be something like the words of Christ in **Rev. 3:15-16**,

> "I know your works: you are neither cold nor hot. Would that you were either cold or hot! So, because you are lukewarm and neither hot nor cold, I will spit you out of my mouth."

You simply cannot have one foot in the church and one foot in the world. You must choose who your Master will be. You cannot love God and the world with the same intensity. **Jam. 4:4**, "...Do you not know that friendship with the world is enmity with God? Therefore, whoever wishes to be a friend of the world makes himself an enemy of God." Sometimes, I wonder, "Is being ashamed of the gospel a betrayal of some kind?"

Chapter 15

He Is Not a Vending Machine God

"For My thoughts are not your thoughts, neither are your ways My ways, declares the Lord. For as the heavens are higher than the earth, so are My ways higher than your ways and My thoughts higher than your thoughts" (**Isa. 55:8-9**).

People often treat God like a vending machine. When you are at work and become hungry, you walk to a vending machine, insert the correct amount of money, and receive your snack in return. You did not think of that vending machine until you were hungry, though, did you? You could walk past it every day and never even notice it – until you are hungry.

That is the way some people treat God, as well. They do not pay Him any attention as they walk through life – past all the beauty of his creation, never even glancing at it. But when they are hungry for something, they fall to their knees and pray fervently that He will accommodate their needs or desires. If they receive what they have asked, they will do exactly what we do after the vending machine gives up its tasty snacks - walk away and not give it another thought until we are hungry again.

Now, let's say you have walked to the machine, inserted the correct number of coins, and chosen your snack of choice. You watch excitedly as the circular "whatever-they-call-it" thing begins to turn, drawing your sweet tooth's prize closer and closer to the end. All that needs to happen now is one more 8th of a turn, and your choice will drop freely to the catch basin. But then your excitement turns to horror as the machine stops whirring, and your candy bar stops tantalizing close to the end but not far enough for it to fall. Panic ensues as you try and shake the heavy machine to dislodge the item. It does not budge.

The panic now turns to fury as you kick the machine, resisting the temptation to curse the owner for "stealing" your hard-earned cash. You walk away, kicking it again and telling everyone what a useless piece of junk that machine is. You even call the owner a cheat and swear you will never use it again. That is, until you are hungry again and need its services once more. That is exactly how people treat God. He is ignored till He is needed and ignored even after the request is granted.

But, let God, in His infinite wisdom, decide not to grant it at all or not precisely at that moment asked for, and the reaction ranges from disappointment to rage. Amid the fury, He is figuratively kicked and insulted by all who will listen. Why would we not be granted our request(s)? Is He powerless or merely "care-less"? What is the point of praying to a God who will not listen to us? Of course, the rage dissipates after a while, and before long, He is forgotten once more – until another need arises.

Chapter 16

Make Sure You Are Not the Stumbling Block

"Therefore, let us not pass judgment on one another any longer, but rather decide never to put a stumbling block or hindrance in any way of a brother" (**Rom. 14:13**).

The second part of this verse is very subjective. Let me give you an example of a situation that perfectly illustrates my point this morning. Many years ago, when I was still a youth minister, some congregation members started clapping during a baptism. The elders in that church did not consider it appropriate, and we respected their authority, teaching the teens not to do so until told otherwise.

Now, before you debate the wrong issue, it is not about the legality of clapping versus not clapping, but instead what happened next. Almost immediately, the blame was laid at the feet of the "rebellious" teens, and they were admonished for something they had no part in. Specifically, they were told that by clapping, they were creating a stumbling block for the mature members of the church. Ultimately, it was proven that the teens were innocent, and the elders were respectful enough to apologize, but a teen then asked a good question.

While they did not clap, why would it not also be considered a stumbling block to those who wanted to clap? Remember, the debate was not about the clapping per se but the fact that what is regarded as a stumbling block for one group could easily be seen as one for the opposing group. The teen argued that the older group is the "power players" in the church, so they automatically and unanimously decide who the stumbling block is, and it is never their peers. He quoted **Rom. 14:1**, "As for the one who is weak in the faith, welcome him, but not to quarrel over opinions."

Now, you can debate "opinion" all you like, but if that is the case, I am afraid you have missed the teen's point. It was an interesting observation by the young lad and one that caused a discussion between the youth group and the elders. What ensued was a respectful discussion between the teens and the elders, who were graciously attentive to the needs of those in their charge. To be clear, the teen was not discussing that exact incident or the authority of the elders. The group was willing to obey them and had done so – they were merely questioning the context of "a stumbling block."

Here is the moral of the story. Be careful not to judge someone as being a stumbling block because you may well be one to them as well. Make sure to use scripture as the only measure for any discussion on who is a hindrance to their fellow Christians. Then, your judgment will be fair, regardless of their age or status in the church.

Chapter 17

Frenemies

"Faithful are the wounds of a friend; profuse are the kisses of an enemy" (**Pro. 27:6**). In life's journey, we will be unfortunate enough to encounter certain individuals who, though professing friendship, may harbor ill intentions. Take note of the words of **Pro. 27:6**, and don't let the spirit of negativity of another person affect your Christianity. There is always going to be some sad or hateful person who will have nothing better to do than ridicule you.

They will bear false witness against you for one reason or another and then try to justify their actions. Their true colors will shine through as they will speak badly of you behind your back while trying to make a half-hearted attempt to your face to be nice. They will try to convince you they are your friend and have your best interests at heart even as they watch you suffer. They will pretend to shed a tear in sympathy for you as you battle the obstacle they placed in your way. They will tell you they "have your back" when, in actual fact, they are the last person you want that close behind you.

They will expect forgiveness and even lament about how "unfair" people have been to them while not being forgiving to you in the slightest. And all this will happen while they remorselessly watch you suffer in the condition they willfully afflicted upon you. Their mantra will be "I am only doing what is best for you." while doing the exact opposite. Their contempt for you will be evidenced by the poorly hidden smirks they cannot hide in their excitement of "getting even."

Maybe you are a threat to their easy existence; perhaps you will confront them when no one else will, or maybe they are trying to hide their sins by wrongfully accusing you of the same or worse. Whatever the case, don't let them steal your joy. People like that have tons of skeletons so large they cannot hide them in the closet for long. The best advice anyone can give you is "keep your eyes open" because their betrayal will be revealed in time. When that happens, leave them "in the rearview mirror," so to speak.

Don't let them steal your joy. Don't let Satan rent space in your head because of their actions. Continue to love, pray, and want the best for them, but have nothing more to do with them. Find loyal friends who genuinely have your best interests at heart and do not want harm to come to you. Take the time to carefully investigate the motives of anyone in your life whom you feel may harbor animosity toward you and rid yourself of them if necessary. Your life will be better for it. Resolve today to find peace and harmony with true friends, not the chaos of "frenemies."

Chapter 18

Grace Is Not an Excuse for Deliberate Sin

As a minister and counselor, I have had individuals sit in my office and try to persuade me that God will not punish them for their willful sins. Of course, the ultimate goal is not so much to convince me as it is to convince themselves that they are "OK" with God despite their deliberate disobedience. One specific example that comes to mind is a young lady living in sin with her boyfriend. They had come to me for help with their relationship but were unhappy with the scriptural admonishment I handed them.

She then took it upon herself to "inform" me of the power of God's grace and mercy. "You don't understand!" the deluded young lady said. "God already knows we are going to get married, so he does not care that we are having sex." It was not only this couple who was guilty of twisting the meaning of God's grace and mercy. Practically every individual who deliberately sins uses the same excuse to justify their choices.

But the Bible is as clear as daylight regarding the matter. **Heb. 10:26** reads as follows,

> "For if we go on sinning deliberately after receiving the knowledge of the truth, there no longer remains a sacrifice for sins, but a fearful expectation of judgment...."

This passage concerns those who realize that only Jesus's sacrifice can pay the hefty price for their salvation. Despite that knowledge, they freely and willfully sin, even though a fearful judgment awaits them.

Christ did not die an agonizing death on the cross to enable sin in our lives but to free us from its devastating effects. In the case of the lady who tried to free her guilty conscience by misinterpreting God's grace, **Rom. 6:1-2** should serve as a stark warning, "What shall we say then? Are we to continue in sin that grace may abound? By no means! How can we who died to sin still live in it?" Paul had just stressed that where sin abounded, grace abounded even more, but he did not want them to misinterpret the effect of grace in relation to continued sin.

Incorrectly trying to prove to me (or herself) that God's grace was more than the sins she and her boyfriend were committing is precisely the point Paul was trying to make in the verses above. Our union with Christ frees us from sin, and the magnitude of that sin is directly related to the extent of God's grace in forgiving it. However, that does not excuse us from doing what we know we ought not to do but continue to do anyway. God's righteous judgment will not forgive our willful ignorance or disobedience of His Word.

There is a saying, "Ignorance of the law is not an excuse," and the same applies to us scripturally. Our ignorance will not save us; only our obedience will. We must put away the excuses and take responsibility for our decisions, purging sin from our lives and glorifying God in our obedience.

Chapter 19

When Someone Asks, "Why Do You Attend Church?"

"And let us consider how to stir up one another to love and good works, not neglecting to meet together, as is the habit of some, but encouraging one another, and all the more as you see the Day drawing near" (**Heb. 10:24-25**).

Going to church is more than merely arriving, attending Bible class and worship, and then leaving again. While those are undoubtedly the primary reasons for attendance, there are others as well. One of the things that makes Sunday service so joyful is that we get to visit with like-minded brothers and sisters. We get to share our victories and defeats over the last week with them and hear about theirs.

In **1Th. 5:11**, Paul tells the church at Thessalonica to "...encourage one another and build one another up, just as you are already doing." Just being able to "vent" about the difficulties we have had or are facing is a massive release for most people. Moreover, being able to do that to people who show genuine care for you and then have appropriate words of encouragement is priceless. Not only are they willing to do that for us, but when things have taken a turn for the worse, they are there to help us. The Galatian church was told to "Bear one another's burdens" (**Gal. 6:2**), and our extended church family is there to do that for us.

I have seen Christians go above and beyond what was expected of them to help a brother or sister in need, whether emotionally, financially, or physically. We all stumble, fall, and succumb to the temptation of sin occasionally. At times we stray from the path of righteousness because of the relentless attacks of the Devil. When that happens, we are often unaware or unable to see how far we have drifted from the Word. In those times, we need someone to point us back to Christ. **Col. 3:16** tells us, "Let the word of Christ dwell in you richly, teaching and admonishing one another in all wisdom."

We need those who love us to care enough about us that they will speak up when we falter. Who better than our church family to do that in love and with spiritual wisdom? Maybe we realize on our own how far sin has dragged us from the loving arms of Christ. In those times, we have our church family to turn to for help. The writer has this to say in **Jam. 5:16**, "Therefore, confess your sins to one another and pray for one another, that you may be healed. The prayer of a righteous person has great power as it is working."

There is nothing more powerful than prayer, nothing more comforting than knowing that someone is praying for us, nothing more capable of helping restore us. So, next time someone asks you why you attend church, you can tell them: to worship God, to remember and reflect on the work of Christ on the cross, to teach and to learn, to love and be loved, to help and be helped, to comfort and be comforted, to admonish and be admonished, and to pray and be prayed for.

Chapter 20

A Fight to the Death

"And I tell you, you are Peter, and on this rock I will build my church, and the gates of hell shall not prevail against it" (**Mat. 16:18**). Not only are we in a personal fight to the death with Satan, but so is the church. This is not new, of course, but it does seem as though the attacks are relentless today. Satan does not fight fair. He is not obvious, and his attacks will often come from within. He never rests because his goal is the utter destruction of the church. We know from Jesus' own words in **Mat. 16:18** that the devil will not succeed. However, that does not mean he will not destroy thousands of churches worldwide. I think we can all agree that the situation is dire now. The prince of darkness seems to have the upper hand, and churches are struggling.

Instead of growing, their numbers are dwindling, and the confused, fear-stricken members stumble around looking tired and worn out. They hope for a revival or look for a numerically stronger church in case the one they attend fails. So, who's at fault? Who is to blame for the struggling church today? We are brothers and sisters; we are. Will our legacy be the collapse of the church – not the death, but the severe shrinking of it? Is this what we are leaving our children? Is the church in its current state because we failed to fight for it? Are we so timid, so shy, so cowardly, or are we simply too afraid to fight the forces that want to tear down the church's walls?

Christ did not stand by and watch us being devoured by the hungry lion in **1Pe. 5:8-9**. He did not have something else to do that was so important that He did not have the time to invest in us. No! Instead of doing nothing, He heroically walked into the arena like a gladiator and took on the enemy face-to-face. He suffered, He bled, and He died – for you and me. But His death was not final. Three days later, he rose and defeated death. In doing so, he dragged us from certain death and clothed us in new whiter-than-white linen.

He did this for you and me, but what have we done in return? Nothing!

We say we are too young, too old, too introverted, too this or too that as excuses for standing idly by. Why aren't we fighting anymore? Why are we cowering in fear in the shadows? Why are we watching from afar, even denying

Him in fear? The insatiable, evil appetite of the devil is devouring the church. There is a song that asks, "Who am I that you, my king, would die for me?" Why, when victory is assured, are we so afraid to step onto the battlefield for Him? What in this world is so threatening to us that we would give up the glory of an eternal home in Heaven? Is what He did not enough? Why, after what He did, do we do nothing?

Do we not realize that the more the church is bruised, the more the world bleeds because the church's health is directly related to the world's health? The fewer Christians there are in the world, the less morality exists, and the more lives and churches Satan drags to the fiery pits of Hell. So, stop making excuses and do something. Prove to God that you are worthy of being called his son or daughter by fighting for the church's life. Pick up the armor of God, step onto the battlefield, and fight Face the heat now so that you don't have to face it in the future.

Chapter 21

Differing Opinions Do Not Create Enemies

"...but in your hearts honor Christ the Lord as holy, always being prepared to make a defense to anyone who asks you for a reason for the hope that is in you; yet do it with gentleness and respect" (**1Pe. 3:15**).

You will never hate someone into the church, and you will never fight them into the church, either. Anger does not convince anyone to accept your point of view. We can clearly see that in politics. When have you ever been angry, screamed at, insulted, or treated someone with hate and then watched them "come around" to your point of view? All you accomplish is to firmly establish a great divide between you and the other person.

I am on many different blogs and church groups on Facebook and the web, and I am often startled at the approach of Christians toward non-believers and each other. It is as if they are fueled with fury, and their vitriolic speech is appalling. They are not led by Christ when they behave that way, but rather by the devil, who wants them to act in such despicable ways toward other people. **Joh. 8:44** is a wake-up call for them, "You are of your father the devil, and your will is to do your father's desires...".

The devil does not want harmony or peace – that does not prosper his agenda. And don't even make the excuse that you are just passionate about your Christianity. That is as ridiculous as someone physically beating you during a political argument because they are "passionate" about their beliefs. If we act like the world, how are we distinguished from them? In **Jo. 15:19,** Jesus said that we are chosen out of the world. What profit is there in spewing execrable things to and about someone with a different opinion? Has that ever gained a friend? **Luk. 6:31** says we should treat people the way we want them to treat us, and I do not know any people who thrive on anger and hatred directed at them.

We should take a different approach, which should be clearly visible to everyone we meet. **Col. 4:6** says, "Let your speech always be gracious, seasoned with salt, so that you may know how you ought to answer each person." Don't follow the angry, hateful person into the trap Satan has successfully lured them into. Be humble and kind. Realize that differing opinions do not create enemies—actions and reactions do.

Chapter 22

Don't Step Out of Your Christianity

"Be sober-minded; be watchful. Your adversary, the devil, prowls around like a roaring lion, seeking someone to devour. Resist him, firm in your faith, knowing that the same kinds of suffering are being experienced by your brotherhood throughout the world" (**1Pe. 5:8-9**).

Too often, people think they can step out of their Christianity and partake in the sins of the world for a fleeting moment. In Africa, a family stopped to photograph a lion that seemed deceptively far away. It was a magnificent specimen with bulging muscles and a beautiful, thick mane, and the temptation to snap a picture was just too great.

The father stepped out and advanced a couple of feet toward the lion for a more precise shot. The car door was open. His family urged him to return to the car's safety, but he ignored them. As he pressed the shutter on the camera, the lion attacked. By the time the father realized what was happening, it was too late. The lion had already covered half the distance and closed in with incredible speed. The father dropped his camera, turned, and ran toward his panicked, screaming family.

They watched in horror, their hands outstretched, trying to pull him to them more quickly with an invisible force. But it was all in vain. He did not reach the safety of the car. The lion pounced on him and dragged him away. A group of park rangers tried to scare away the lion and even parked their vehicle over the unfortunate man to dissuade the attack. It worked. The lion was defeated and ran off, but not before ending the unfortunate man's life. The family's agony as they watched in horror while the lion devoured their loved one was unimaginable.

Don't step out of your Christianity to enjoy the fleeting, sinful "joys" of the world. The devil is prowling around, waiting for you to leave the safety of Christ so that he can devour you. You will not always make it back to safety and the outstretched arms of friends and family who are begging you to return.

Strangers may come to your aid and fight for you, but it might be too late. Your death will be agonizing for those you love as they watch sin devour you. Don't step out of your Christianity. Stay where it is safe.

Don't let what is intriguing but dangerous tempt you to get out. The devil is always deceptively close and waiting. Look through the closed window at the ugliness of sin and drive away – and fight for those who have made the mistake you did not. "...let him know that whoever brings back a sinner from his wandering will save his soul from death and will cover a multitude of sins." (**Jam. 5:20**).

Chapter 23

Just Don't Say, "Keep Christ in Christmas"

"...It is more blessed to give than to receive" (**Act. 20:35**). As we approach the holiday season, we will do well to remember those words spoken by Jesus and quoted by Paul the Apostle. For most people in the world, the "season of giving" is more about receiving than anything else. Think carefully about Christmas Day. From now until December 25, millions of people worldwide begin to dream of the gifts they will receive. They will tell parents and loved ones what they want and write letters to "Santa" requesting gift after gift. As the day draws ever closer, they will begin to fixate on the presents under the tree, picking them up and shaking them to see if they can guess what it is.

Sleep will be hard on Christmas Eve. Children will want to see Santa or simply cannot wait to open the presents. They will get up Early in the morning and run to the tree or their parents' room to wake them up. Tired parents will drag themselves out of bed and go to watch as their loved ones open gift after gift after gift. Shouts of glee will express satisfaction as gift bags, paper, boxes, and bows litter the room. The festive mood will continue as games are played and food is prepared, some of which was begun the day before. By lunchtime, everyone will be hungry and ready to partake in a sumptuous feast of meats, vegetables, and favorite desserts. Too much will be eaten before returning to the gifts, games, or television to watch some sport.

Later that day, some will return for "seconds" before watching classic Christmas movies and retiring to bed. Santa outdid himself, and exhausted parents and children begin to look forward to New Year's Eve. Now, I ask an obvious question: "What is missing from this story?" "Avarice, gluttony, and slothfulness" abound on that day, but very little, if any, mention is made of Christ. Would He want us to act that way? Would He be happy if we woke up on "His birthday," as many believe it to be, and never mentioned Him? People sing, scream, and shout, "Keep Christ in Christmas," and then ignore him, or at best, give Him a fleeting mention at lunchtime.

If you believe that is His day, why do you exclude Him? Would He not want you to share your spoils with the millions who will not have access to warm meals, gifts, or even a roof over their heads? Listen, buy gifts, open presents, eat, and rest. Show love to your family and friends, but don't pretend to make it about Him when you act in ways that shame His name. Enjoy the fruits of your labor, the joy of giving to those you love, but remember, "...it is more blessed to give than to receive" applies to more than just your immediate family.

As for keeping Christ in Christmas, leave Christmas to Santa and keep Christ in every day of the year. Honor Him by sharing your measure of wealth with those who would happily eat the crumbs off your floor or play with your child's old, broken toys. Just don't say "Keep Christ in Christmas" and then ignore Him by acting like the world – or worse.

Chapter 24
Without This Day

"Rejoice always, pray without ceasing, give thanks in all circumstances; for this is the will of God in Christ Jesus for you" (**1Th. 5:16-18**). On Thanksgiving Day, many people in the USA will gather with family and friends to watch sports, play games, or enjoy each other's company. At mealtime, we will give thanks for the many blessings in our lives before partaking in a hearty meal (a great blessing itself). Of course, there are many things to be thankful for, but how many people spend any time thanking God for all the blessings in their lives?

It is not that we should not be grateful for all other good things in our lives – we absolutely should, but we should not forget the source of every single one of them. **Jam. 1:17** puts it this way, "Every good gift and every perfect gift is from above, coming down from the Father of lights, with whom there is no variation or shadow due to change." Nothing good comes from anywhere else. It might come to us by the hands of man, but it originated in one place only. No matter where we live, no matter our circumstances, our victory over the devil has already been secured, and we should be grateful for that every single day of our lives. Is there any greater blessing than that?

So, enjoy your day with those you love. Remember those who cooked the food and will clean the dishes. Be thankful for those who have gone before us, who gave their lives in defense of the gospel, and those who did so to ensure our freedoms. Please take a moment to be grateful to those serving in the military, the police force, firefighters, and the medical field whose lives are on the line daily to ensure our safety. Don't forget those who keep our streets clean, those who pick up the garbage so we can have clean, disease-free neighborhoods, those who do all the other "forgotten" jobs that we would not or could never do, and those who are working while we are resting.

Take a moment to be thankful for teachers who train our children in the knowledge of the world and the church for teaching them in the wisdom of the Lord. Be grateful to those whose lives are at risk every day as they take the gospel to people in need in places where preaching it is life-threatening. Take a moment and give thanks for your measure of health and wealth, for friends and family who love you. Give thanks for whatever has made your life what it is today, but above all, thank God for today because "This is the day the Lord has made; let us rejoice and be glad in it." (**Psa. 118:24**). Remember, without this day; you would not be able to be thankful for anything.

Chapter 25
God's Discipline

"O LORD, rebuke me not in your anger, nor discipline me in your wrath. Be gracious to me, O LORD, for I am languishing; heal me, O LORD, for my bones are troubled. My soul also is greatly troubled...Depart from me, all you workers of evil, for the LORD has heard the sound of my weeping. The LORD has heard my plea; the LORD accepts my prayer. All my enemies shall be ashamed and greatly troubled; they shall turn back and be put to shame in a moment" (**Psa. 6:1-10**).

We do not know the occasion of David's languishing, but he certainly believed that he was under God's rebuke.

God's discipline was not for the sake of wrath but rather an act of great love. **Heb. 12:5-6** has this to say about God's punishment,

"...My son, do not regard lightly the discipline of the Lord, nor be weary when reproved by him. For the Lord disciplines the one he loves and chastises every son whom he receives."

It is for discipline that you must endure. God is treating you as sons. For what son is there whom his father does not discipline?" God also disciplines us because we are His children, and He loves us. It gives Him no pleasure, but getting our attention and redirecting us is necessary. Like David, we sometimes lament, blaming others and maybe even God Himself for our situation, when instead, we should be looking inward.

Just like an addict must first admit their addiction before healing can occur, we too must utter those words for ours to begin. We must realize why we are in a pickle, and if we are to blame, we must correct it. Sometimes, it takes physical and spiritual trials to make us come to our senses. Then, when we arrive at that place, we need to utter the words, "Depart from me, you workers of evil," and banish those sins (or people) from our lives. It may be challenging, but we must decide what's more important – those earthly friends and sin – or God. **Jam. 4:4** states,

> "You adulterous people! Do you not know that friendship with the world is enmity with God? Therefore, whoever wishes to be a friend of the world makes himself an enemy of God."

Choose your friends carefully because it has everlasting consequences. Be like the boxer in Halifax, England, as told by Edwin Orr at the turn of the century. He was a champion and wanted to convert to Christianity, but his friends ridiculed him. They told him he would have to choose Christ or the championship belt. This was his reply, "I'll both give it up and you up! If you won't go with me to heaven, I won't go with you to hell!" The choice should be a simple one. Realize your mistakes, cast away your bad friendships and sin, repent, and be reconciled to God through Christ Jesus, His Son. It is worth it in the long run.

Chapter 26
The Only Way to Be That Blind

I saw a post on Facebook a while back that got me riled up. There are a lot of those on FB – posts that are meant to elicit some reaction, but I mostly ignore them. Not this one, though; this one got under my skin. It was a meme that stated, "It doesn't matter how many Sundays you sit in church or if you think you are saved. God sees what you do and how you treat people. That's what really matters. Amen." The deluded soul who wrote this actually dared to end it with "Amen." Really?

First, Sunday service won't guarantee your entry into heaven, but it will go a long way to ensuring you are preparing yourself. For Christians who say, "We don't have to go to church.", I have this to say in reply, "**Phm. 1:2; 1Co. 16:5, 1Co. 16:19; Mat. 18:20; Col. 4:15, 1Co. 14:26; Act. 13:1; Mat. 18:17** and **Act. 12:5**, and those are just a few I mentioned here. Moreover, to whom were many of the epistles written? Did they read those letters in the town square or the presence of several Christians at a specific location? Of course, the Church is not a physical building; no one argues that.

But no one can earnestly contend that Christians have not always come together in a specific location to worship God, whether in a home, in a building or other structure, in an open field, or under a tree. And let's not forget the words of **Heb. 10:25**, "Not neglecting to meet, as is the habit of some, but encouraging one another...." I have written devotionals and delivered sermons on the benefits of attending church services beyond listening to a sermon. The second point I want to address was even more infuriating because the individual stated that it does not matter if you think you are saved – the only thing that matters is what you do and how you treat others. I don't "think" I have been saved; I "know" I have been saved.

The Word of God assures me of this. **1Jo 5:13**, "I write these things to you who believe in the name of the Son of God, that you may know that you have eternal life." Accepting God's word and obedience to it saves me, so it is not only about how I treat others. Does it matter that I treat others with empathy, respect, and love? Of course, it does. **Mar. 12:31**, "You shall love your neighbor as yourself," and **Mat. 22:37-39**,

> "...You shall love the Lord your God with all your heart and with all your soul and with all your mind. This is the great and first commandment. And the second is like it: You shall love your neighbor as yourself."

But that alone is definitely not enough to save you; I can guarantee you that. People who believe that only loving people will save you are not free of the responsibility and accountability of obedience to all of God's other commandments, as John declares in **Joh. 14:15**, "If you love me, you will keep my commandments."

Chapter 27

Supplement Your Faith From This Moment On

"For this very reason, make every effort to supplement your faith with virtue, and virtue with knowledge, and knowledge with self-control, and self-control with steadfastness, and steadfastness with godliness, and godliness with brotherly affection, and brotherly affection with love. For if these qualities are yours and are increasing, they keep you from being ineffective or unfruitful in the knowledge of our Lord Jesus Christ.

For whoever lacks these qualities is so nearsighted that he is blind, having forgotten that he was cleansed from his former sins. Therefore, brothers, be all the more diligent in confirming your calling and election, for if you practice these qualities, you will never fall. For in this way there will be richly provided for you an entrance into the eternal kingdom of our Lord and Savior Jesus Christ" (**2Pe. 1:5-11**).

"Virtue" – high moral standard; "knowledge" – facts gained from studious behavior; "self-control" – exercising restraint over one's passions and desires; "steadfastness" – being resolutely firm and unwavering; "godliness" – being devoutly religious; "brotherly affection" – gently feeling of fondness/liking, "love" – an intense feeling of affection accompanied with devotion. These are the things Peter says will keep us from being "ineffective or unfruitful" in our Christian pursuit. Too often, we put on Christ in baptism and then sit back and wait for the glorious first-class coach to transport us to the doors of heaven.

We think we have reached the pinnacle of our faith, and nothing more is required of us beyond the most basic actions to maintain our "saved" status. But that is not the case. Most industries expect (and some even require) periodic training to increase knowledge and effectiveness, and the same can be said for our Christianity. The state you are in today should never be the same as the one you are in tomorrow. You should make it your primary goal to increase the things of the Spirit to better yourself because not doing so makes you so nearsighted that you are blind.

Failure to stay in the Word and grow in knowledge will soon lead to complacency, which can lead to laziness, weakness, and an inability to resist temptation and sin. However, if you pursue spiritual knowledge, you will be able to guard yourself against the devil's wily ways and not stumble and fall. Then, you will be successful in being virtuous and gain knowledge that will lead to self-control and steadfast faithfulness.

In turn, you will increase your godliness as much as possible and have a greater love for your fellow man. And then, as Peter puts it, "...there will be richly provided for you an entrance into the eternal kingdom of our Lord and Savior Jesus Christ." So, supplement your faith from this moment on.

Chapter 28

Not a Resolution, But a Wish with a Prayer

"I, therefore, a prisoner for the Lord, urge you to walk in a manner worthy of the calling to which you have been called, with all humility and gentleness, with patience, bearing with one another in love, eager to maintain the unity of the Spirit in the bond of peace" (**Eph. 4:1-3**).

If this article sounds familiar to some of you, it is because I wrote a similar one not too long ago, but the topic is so perplexing that I wanted to address it again. Millions of people worldwide will reflect on the past year, remembering both the happy and sad events of last year.

They will probably make the obligatory New Year's resolutions and excitedly wait for the "dropping of the ball" to enthusiastically wish each other a happy and prosperous coming year. Amongst all the excitement and anticipation, most of us will wonder if we will finally rid ourselves of the curse of COVID and return to whatever we consider normality. I do not have a New Year's resolution as much as a wish this year – a wish that is accompanied by a sincere prayer. Many years ago, I invited a close friend to church services, and his response was puzzling to me at the time. He emphatically stated that he would never attend church services because "You guys cannot even get along. I do not want to be around so much hate."

This year, I have come to understand what he meant by that, even if his logic was a little flawed. You see, most Christians are peaceable, loving each other with grace and kindness and concentrating on making themselves more acceptable in His sight. But far too many spend their time denigrating other believers, and I want to address that problem today with my New Year's wish. My wish is that we will have patience with one another and treat each other with love and gentleness. Social media has been a great source of education and entertainment for the world, but it has also been a vehicle of anger and even hate for some individuals.

I am on many different platforms, social media, and blogging sites. On most of them, some individuals act with such fierce anger at another person's differing opinion that it is hard to see Christianity in any of it. I am not sure if they understand their effect on people who come across like that, where bickering becomes arguments, and arguments become disparaging words filled with hatred. What newcomers see is a violent ideology and hate-filled speech, not loving Christ-followers having a purposeful, respectful debate. Baptists hating Catholics, Catholics hating Pentecostals, Pentecostals hating the Church of Christ, the Church of Christ hating Presbyterians, Presbyterians hating some other tradition, etc.

Where is the love you are commanded to have for one another? Are you so focused on fighting someone to your point of view that you don't read and obey scriptures like **Mar. 12:31**, "You shall love your neighbor as yourself?" Have your belief and stand firm on it, but for the sake of unity, especially for those who are searching, have a modicum of respect for each other. Have a lively, passionate debate, but don't allow that to turn into hatred because the other person is "too stupid to see your point of view." And please, stop saying "all of you" when you don't know every person in that group.

I experimented not too long ago to see if there was any return to respect after allowing fierce and frankly disrespectful arguments to occur. I found almost no chance of that. Once the ship of love and respect sails, apparently, it loses its way in the storms of anger and hatred. Have enough love for each other that you do not allow your passions to dictate your attitude. Realize that your words are not an encouragement to most people hearing them. If you find yourself in a disrespectful "fight," exit it. People who are searching will not be encouraged to attend church if no love is shown to each other by those who claim to follow Christ.

Chapter 29

Show Me the Scripture

After a recent online post, at least two concerned readers questioned my youth ministry reference. They both commented similarly and asked me to show them scriptures to defend youth ministers. The Bible does not explicitly mention youth ministers. However, over time, the church realized the enormous pressure modern society was having on teens, and as a result, youth ministry developed. The spiritual needs of "children" are the same as those of adults, but the approach differs.

Allow me to recall my experience, which I am sure mirrors many who filled or are filling that position in a church somewhere in the world. More than 20 kids were baptized as a direct result of that ministry. They came because someone in the group invited them to spend time with them and attend worship. Would they have come if there was no youth group where they could first go and be approached in a specific way? I called most of them yesterday, and five said they would have attended with a friend, irrespective of the youth group. Two were not sure. I could not contact two others, leaving eleven (assuming the two sides with the previous group).

Eleven saved souls as a direct result of the youth group. One of them attended two preaching schools and is a successful minister today. Of course, they (opponents) would claim that there is no scripture for ministers either, but that does not change the fact that he is saved. In fact, except for the two I failed to contact, all eighteen are faithful to this day. I am unsure if you know the statistics, but that is a remarkable rate of faithfulness. So, as I said to one reader, I will never apologize for my time as a youth minister.

Our group directly caused them to study and put Christ on in baptism. And, for those who used the youth group to escape the daily misery at home and find solace and safety there – what of them? But I have a question for the opponents – will you tell those young adults their baptism was invalid? I have a few more questions for you. Some may apply to you specifically, and some may not, but feel free to correct my erroneous thought with scripture for all of the following. Show me scriptures that specifically address song leaders. Or show me scriptures that address PowerPoint.

What about Bible study before service or Wednesday evening study? How about scriptures that address church buildings outside of the home? What about a woman speaking in church? Do you allow your ladies to share their opinions outside the auditorium but still within the confines of the "building"? While you are at it, show the scriptures for classrooms, foyers, etc. What about seminars, counseling, or other activities in the church? Address some or all of them. Some are there to make it easier to attend services; some are not.

But here is the biggest and by far the most important statement/question for you, and I would prefer you to defend this one with scripture first. If you are on the Internet – then you are on what is arguably the most licentious, most "evil" platform ever to have been introduced to humanity. Even as you read this, hate is being spewed out on it; millions of men, women, and children are watching pornography and other evils. Please show me the scripture to defend the group you are currently on, including Facebook. Don't be selective and draw a circle of righteousness around yourself and your minimalistic scriptural practices while you support one of the richest, anti-Christian platforms on the Internet.

The Internet contains satanism, openly licentious sites, pornography, and evolution, to name but a few tools Satan can use to draw the weak away from the loving arms of God. Despite what you think, we will continue to do whatever is in our power, using all the modern tools available to us to reach those who are lost in sin.

Chapter 30

When You Get the Call at 3 AM

Usually, I respond to a few of the thousands of comments I receive from the various groups, blogs, and platforms I post my articles to, and then move on. They are meant to encourage and create a conversation so that we all can learn, and for the most part, we do. But now and then, I feel the need to return to one. But before I do, let me apologize. I always called my old youth group members "my kids," and I still do, so I unintentionally used that word when speaking of baptisms. I am sorry for the confusion. I did not baptize children.

I want to address youth ministry briefly this morning using two examples. I respect everyone's view and know we will unlikely jump over to the other side, so this is only for explanation purposes. As a trained minister and a qualified counselor, I could effectively minister to the youth at our church (and other churches). I am not saying that parents cannot fulfill some of those roles, but are they not similarly ministering to the youth if they do? Anyway, here are the stories (with their permission): One individual had done something when she was 14 that she could not forgive herself for. She could not bring herself to admit her mistake to her parents, and her friends were not qualified to minister to what she had done.

Guilt consumed her, and she felt God would not forgive her. She did not want to approach adults because she knew (in her mind) that they would tell her parents or condemn her. The second individual had self-esteem issues exacerbated by her being bullied in school. The officials at her school did nothing beyond a bit of discipline to end the bullying. It did not stop. She approached adults in the church and was given sound advice, "Tell your parents and school officials." But that was insufficient. She had learned to bottle the feelings, but it was becoming overwhelming, and she wanted it all to "just go away." Both girls reached out to me because of the relationship we had (and still have to this day).

What few people understand is the loving bond that is developed between youth ministers and their groups. Six years after my time as a youth minister, I am still called "2nd Dad" and occasionally give them advice. I provided those two "kids" guidance and walked through the storm with them. At the right time, we informed their parents and authorities of the situation, and I stayed until the storm had subsided. We walked, sat, spoke, cried, laughed, and encouraged each other. To this day, I receive cards and letters thanking me because - these are their words, "I would not be here if I did not have you in my life."

Of course, there are concerned, and even qualified parents and adults these kids can turn to, but the relationships we develop(ed) with them are so close that they know we have their backs even as we persuade them to do the right thing. There is much more to these stories than I can recount here and more that I could use as examples, but I only have this to say. If the time I spent at soccer, baseball, school plays, camp, on retreats, in class, in personal Bible studies, etc., was of such a benefit that I could save them from the darkness they experienced, I will never apologize. Maybe we should forgo the title "Youth Minister," but even if we do, someone will fulfill all or part of that ministry anyway.

Chapter 31
Striving for Unity

"I appeal to you, brothers, by the name of our Lord Jesus Christ, that all of you agree, and that there be no divisions among you, but that you be united in the same mind and the same judgment" (**1Co. 1:10**).

Near the end of his third missionary journey, approximately seven years after he and his companions founded the church (**Act. 18**), Paul wrote this letter to them – a church that was in a fair amount of trouble. Corinth was the main land route from the East to the West, where several sea routes converged, but it was also known for its utterly pagan society.

Although Paul begins the letter positively, it does not take him long before he plunges into an analysis of their wrongdoings. First Corinthians is one of Paul's most reasoned epistles, and with careful reading, one can follow his line of thinking accurately. Paul's analysis and conclusion about the Corinthian church could just as easily be applied to many churches today. He begins with division in the church (**vs. 1-4**) and continues discussing discipline (**vs. 5-6**), marriage and divorce (**v. 7**), doctrinal disputes (**vs. 8-10**), and misunderstanding spiritual gifts.

He also examines incorrect worship services regarding the Lord's Supper, women's role, and the resurrection. Paul is beginning a discussion on the division of the church and wants them to know that it is not proper for Christians to have the type of attitude that is not united. He says they should be "in the same mind," which tells us the importance of church unity and contentment. Today, the lesson is equally important as divisions seem to plague many US and world congregations. With over 300 denominations in America alone and thousands more worldwide, there is a complete lack of being of the "same mind and judgment."

People read the Bible with a presupposed conclusion and interpretation. To be unified, in one mind, and with the same judgment, we need to allow the Word to speak to us and not fight over the terminology. If you look at the state of the Corinthian church with all that was going on (or not going on), you can see that even from the beginning, men were coming in with their versions of what should or should not be happening. This was not the only letter that spoke to the issue of unity. A similar call for unity is expressed in Ephesians, while in Galatians, a warning is proclaimed to those who would twist the Word of God – **Gal. 1:8**, "But even if we or an angel from heaven should preach to you a gospel contrary to the one we preached to you, let him be accursed."

The best we can do is check all the time - Check what the preacher has said (**Act. 17:11**) and test the spirits to see whether what he said is from God (**1Jo. 4:1**). No one is immune to making mistakes, but when the "errors" are intentional, we need to find another place where God's truth is preached as delivered and not from man's limited reasoning.

Chapter 32

Don't Allow the Devil to Dictate Your Outcome

"I can do all things through Him who strengthens me" (**Php. 4:13**). There are times when you are driven to your knees in despair. These are times when the impossible seems to have happened, and solutions are far away. Problems and trials have risen like an unconquerable mountain, and fear and desperation have overcome you. Sometimes, it may even seem as if the solutions will never come. Every agonizing step drains you even more, and you are scared and tired. Depression takes the place of joy, and the future begins to look hopeless.

Even in our darkest hour, though, there is hope. A hope predicated on our belief that we are not alone and that God will keep his promise in **Heb. 13:6** never to leave or forsake us; a belief that we can do all things and therefore overcome all of life's challenges with "Him who strengthens" us. Our outcome was not predetermined by a God who chose this person or that one to be His elect. Instead, that same God gave us time, intelligence, and choice to make the final destination one of our own choosing.

That said, there will be times, those times on your knees when the universe seems to be conspiring against you, when the pain and suffering of this brief moment we call life overtakes you, when you may secretly wish for the end to come quickly. You may even feel like death would be a welcome relief from all the uncertainty, pain, and anguish you are experiencing. During that moment, please don't give in to it. Instead, look up, close your eyes, and pray. Ask for the strength to persevere, take the punches, and continue in faith because you are not alone. You have God, the loving and merciful Creator, on your side.

Some professionals are knowledgeable and experienced in helping souls when they feel at their wits' end. You have friends, family, and even strangers praying for you and who are willing to help you. You have people who are inspired by what you do and who you are. They need your love, your kindness, and your support when they are in pain. The strength you show during your suffering may be the only thing that inspires them to fight. Your victory will inspire theirs. Think of them and fight for yourself and them. You do not belong to some weak god who promises everything and delivers nothing.

You belong to a God who is omnipotent. You will overcome because you have Christ in your heart, and all things are possible with Him. Your outcome will not always be what you desire, but you will not fight alone, and you will persevere until He calls you home. In the meantime, we will have the gift of your precious life, smile, hugs, and love for a treasured while longer. And remember, when you have those specific thoughts, understand it is not God calling you home, but something more sinister, more evil, that wants to separate you from your God. Don't give in – don't allow the devil to determine your outcome.

Chapter 33

Just Be Like an Ant

"Go to the ant, O sluggard; consider her ways and be wise. Without having any chief, officer, or ruler, she prepares her bread in summer and gathers her food in harvest. How long will you lie there, O sluggard? When will you arise from your sleep?" (**Pro. 6:6-9**).

Have you ever watched a colony of ants at work? They are selfless and place the survival of the colony above themselves. Each individual ant has a role to play in the larger scheme of things, and they never argue or shirk their responsibility. If you have ever sat and observed them, you would quickly notice how hardworking they are – never stopping until the task at hand is complete. The writer of this proverb uses the analogy of an ant when referring to man's productivity.

We live in a world that teaches us that we are the only thing that matters. Our happiness is all that counts. The only thing that matters is satisfying our selfish desires. As a result, many people have also become increasingly lazy. They expect life's pleasures to come to them without any toil on their part. These entitled individuals believe that they are owed something merely because they exist. Instead of being conquerors, they have the attitude of, "Well, I did not ask to be born, so it is your responsibility to take care of me." "No!" says the writer emphatically. He wants his readers, especially those who are sluggards, to "Go to the ant...." We all know how hard ants work, not only for themselves but also for the greater good of the colony.

They have a role to play and do it without hesitation or complaint. I have yet to see an ant drop something five times the size of their body so that they can complain about how "overworked" they are or how insufficient rewards are. I am not saying that those complaints are never justified because there are occasions where that is absolutely the case. I am speaking of the sluggard - the person unwilling to lift a finger because they are too exhausted, too sick, too busy watching something on TV, or too engrossed in some mindless video game to get anything done. They are the "I'll do it tomorrow" group of people who sit around and do nothing and then complain because nothing is getting done.

How many people do you know who will use any number of excuses to pass the work on to others? How many people do you know who spend far too many hours sleeping and far too few accomplishing anything of value? In some ways, our spiritual lives are the same. Either we sleep in the darkness or walk in the light. There will come a time to rest, but that is not now. Jesus said in **Joh. 9:4**, "We must work the works of him who sent me while it is day; night is coming when no one can work." This is the time to work the ground, to plant and harvest, the season to get things done before rest comes. You are working not only for yourself but for the kingdom of God, and you do not want to be found wanting when the rewards are handed out. Work now and rest in Heaven forever.

Chapter 34

Are You a Treasure or a Rotten Apple?

"Blessed is the man who walks not in the counsel of the wicked, nor stands in the way of sinners, nor sits in the seat of scoffers, but his delight is in the law of the Lord, and on his law, he meditates day and night. He is like a tree planted by streams of water that yields its fruit in its season, and its leaf does not wither. In all that he does, he prospers" (**Psa. 1:1-3**).

What kind of man are you? I know men that are honorable and strong. Their loyalty to God and their family is beyond question. When you see how they treat the love of their life, you cannot but admire them. They do not belittle, denigrate, or mock but instead encourage with both words and actions.

They understand the value of a loving wife and are proud to be called her husband. They desire to bring up their children in the way of the Lord, and that is always at the heart of their relationship with them. They observe and delight in the small things their kids do and are always available for school events. They are never afraid to play childish games with them because they know the importance of their presence. They encourage them with love and words of affirmation and their lives are examples of devoted Christians to all who know them. They are not afraid to discipline but do so only when necessary and in a manner appropriate for the situation. Every night witnesses them on their knees, praying fervently for every family member and their friends.

This kind of man protects those he loves with fierce determination and is not afraid to die for them if necessary. They can usually be seen with a Bible in their hand, and everything they do is directed by it. They are not ashamed of displaying their love, and a hug and a kiss are always available; their strong arms a refuge to their children and their wives when they are afraid. They are the epitome of courage, integrity, and trustworthiness, and more than once, you will hear someone say, "I want to be like him when I grow up." But I also know the opposite of this man. Those men are angry, afraid they will not be seen as "strong," and will use any means necessary to be seen as such. Screaming, cursing, and hatred are liberally spewed out in an attempt to take control of everyone forcefully.

They are not loved but feared, and compliance with them is not willing or out of respect but to prevent overly harsh consequences. They respect no opinion besides their own, and they never utter the word "sorry." They often can be heard boasting about their female conquests even though they are married and delight in sinful and immoral practices. They don't encourage but rather constantly scold, berate, and tear down, replacing their victim's self-confidence with insecurity and doubt. They find fault with everything and everyone and are never satisfied with anything. They thrive on forced control, and punishment is self-empowering. Unfortunately for their victim, the harsher the punishment, the more satisfied and empowered they feel. They think they are "all that," but they are not.

They are weak, afraid, self-centered bullies who have no empathy and little to no self-control. They are disloyal, bear false witness, display no integrity, and are untrustworthy. No one wants to be like them, and few call them "friend." Do people delight in your presence or fear it? Will they treasure your memory until the day they die, or discard it like a rotten apple and never think of it again?

Chapter 35

The Reward Far Outweighs the Sacrifice

"If then you have been raised with Christ, seek the things that are above, where Christ is, seated at the right hand of God. Set your mind on things that are above, not on things that are on earth" (**Col. 3:1-2**).

A similar thought is found in **Rom. 8:5**, "Those who live according to the flesh set their minds on the flesh; but those who live according to the Spirit set their minds on the things of the Spirit." A Christian who has been raised with Christ cannot hold on to the things of the world and still claim to be a son or daughter of God.

Not all the things of the world are evil, but the Devil will try to use all of them to draw your attention away from God. When you see a person you desire to be with, it leads to love and marriage. Obviously, nothing is wrong with that...it is a natural part of life. But, when you are already in a committed relationship, desiring someone else is not good. That kind of desire leads to adultery if you or they are married or dishonesty if you are in a dating relationship.

Another example is money. There is nothing inherently wrong with seeking money to live comfortably. That is why you go to college or university or take an apprenticeship. You want to provide for your family, so instead of being evil, that is honorable. However, when the drive to earn money becomes an obsession, and you put it in front of your spiritual life, it leads to all sorts of evil. **1Ti. 6:9-11**,

"But those who desire to be rich fall into temptation, into a snare, into many senseless and harmful desires that plunge people into ruin and destruction. For the love of money is the root of all kinds of evils. It is through this craving that some have wandered away from the faith and pierced themselves with many pangs. But as for you, O man of God, flee these things. Pursue righteousness, godliness, faith, love, steadfastness, gentleness."

Clearly, we see that there are many good things that the Devil can use to distract you from your mission to be an honorable, dedicated Christian. Too often, we allow our desires to turn into obsessions and, in doing so, dishonor ourselves with our words and actions. For those who struggle to decide what is good and evil, a good rule of thumb is this: if it is self-centered, self-seeking, and spiritually destructive, it is bad – even if it began as a good thing.

Rom. 1:18-32 and **Gal. 5:19-21** lists some of the things that we should strive to put off, and **Col. 3:5** describes the categories of earthly things we should rid ourselves of: "Put to death what is earthly in you: sexual immorality, impurity, passion, evil desire, and covetousness, which is idolatry." By contrast, what we should set our minds on is given to us in **Col. 3:12**, "Put on then, as God's chosen ones, holy and beloved, compassionate hearts, kindness, humility, meekness, and patience." Is it easy to do that? Of course not. Nothing worthwhile ever is, but the reward for being a diligent, obedient child of God far outweighs the "sacrifice" of leaving the things of the world behind. The reward far outweighs the sacrifice.

Chapter 36

He Knows the Future – We Do Not

"Trust in the Lord with all your heart, and do not lean on your own understanding. In all your ways acknowledge him, and he will make straight your paths" (**Pro. 3:5-6**).

Has an individual ever approached you with a question like whether they should change the security of a job for the uncertainty of a better-paying one somewhere else? Maybe they wanted to know if they should leave a dating partner because they have violent tendencies or are suspected of infidelity. Did you sit them down and give them the best advice you can think of, only to have them ignore you? Did you find that annoying?

It is even more annoying when it is one of our children. We have lived through the things they are experiencing, and we want to protect them. We want to pass on our wealth of lessons learned in the "school of hard knocks," but they don't listen. They do not trust us because they think they know better. They may even agree with us when we are giving the advice, but no sooner do we leave than they resort to their own "understanding" – sometimes with disastrous results. Who among us does not find that incredibly annoying? If only they had listened and not been so arrogant as to think they knew better.

If only they trusted our wise words of wisdom. Maybe they would have been spared the pain if only they had listened to our sound advice. How often have you asked God for direction, only to ignore it because you did not like the answer? "God," you say, "I think you may have misunderstood the question, so let me ask it again." When the answer does not change, we throw out the Creator's advice and "go it alone" – sometimes with disastrous results. The fact of the matter is that we tend to mistrust any advice that does not match our desired solution. It seems safer to lean on our own understanding and do what we think is best for us.

After all, who knows better what is best for us than ourselves? We only ask others, including God, for their advice to affirm what we already intend to do. So, when we do not receive the desired answer, we think they do not understand the question, do not see it from our perspective, or worse still, are trying to harm us. Trusting our parents or friends takes a leap of faith, but trusting God takes an enormous leap because we do not physically see or audibly hear Him. But His advice, given to us through the word, our conscience, or common sense, is always the best because He sees what we do not.

If our parents know more than we do because they have experienced what we are currently going through, how much more does God know? Did he not create our parents? Was He not around from the beginning of humanity? Is He not omniscient (all-knowing)? God wants to direct our paths because He has a plan for us. **Jer. 29:11** "For I know the plans I have for you, declares the Lord, plans for welfare and not for evil, to give you a future and a hope." If we believe in God, surely we should be able to trust that He has the best solution. Do we not think He knows what's best for us because He knows the future and we do not?

Chapter 37
The Absurdity of Atheism

"In the beginning, God created the heavens and the earth. The earth was without form and void, and darkness was over the face of the deep. And the Spirit of God was hovering over the face of the waters" (**Gen. 1:1-2**).

An atheist will tell you that you are stupid for believing a God you cannot prove exists despite evidence to the contrary – while believing this: Once, there was nothing (the absence of anything). One day, nothing suddenly became something with no external influence. In the newly created space, which they cannot explain, particles started moving at tremendously high speeds, in different directions, no less. This happened without any external motivating force.

One day, two of these particles collided with enough power that, under normal circumstances, would obliterate everything. Instead, they created trillions of planets in billions of galaxies. One of those planets just happened to be the exact distance from its sun, with enough layers of atmosphere to sustain life (which did not exist). As the planet cooled, water was created. In these vast, created seas, life magically began (without an external creator). These tiny, single-living cells were discontent with their limited lifestyle (even though they did not develop an actual thinking brain). One day, they thought (even though they couldn't), "I am tired of being a single cell. It will take millions of years, but I will learn to move around".

So they developed fins and things and swam (even though they had no food initially). Anyway, it did not take long in the grand scheme of time for them to be unhappy again, so they thought, "We would like to soar in the heavens," so they jumped out of the water enough time to grow wings, feathers, and working birdy parts to fly. Oh, and they had to learn to eat seeds and things. But not every fish wanted to fly in the heavens, so they decided to walk on the earth, so they developed paws, lungs, and stuff. But they were hungry, so some ate leaves, but others thought their friends looked tastier, so they ate them.

Then they realized they were not intelligent, so they thought they would grow a brain and, at the same time, walk on two feet because all that walking on all fours was not fun at all. The newly formed monkeys were cold, though, because winters were brutal since there weren't enough cows or humanity to create the global warming phenomenon, so they made fire and lived in caves. They found fire only warmed them when they were near the fire, so they killed their cousins and made coats. They realized their extended family tasted really good when cooked, so they killed and ate them.

Of course, they were not happy walking, so they invented the wheel, but not before they hated too much hair and asked nature to shave it. Then they became man because they did not want to be referred to as "ape-men," and here we are. But, not all fish wished to leave the confines of the water, and not all monkeys wanted to be man, so that is why there are still fish and animals and monkeys. Now, that takes faith – and they ridicule you for yours. If there is no God, they will never get to say, "Told you so!" because they could only say that after we both die, and since we simply cease to exist, there will be no conscious thoughts. But what if we are correct? Where does that leave them?

Chapter 38

Unforgiveness: The Anchor That Drowns Your Joy

"Pay attention to yourselves! If your brother sins, rebuke him, and if he repents, forgive him, and if he sins against you seven times in the day, and turns to you seven times, saying, 'I repent, you must forgive him" (**Luk. 17:3-4**).

If I asked you what the most challenging thing for a Christian to do is, what would you say? If we are honest with ourselves, most of us would say "to forgive." We all know forgiving someone we feel has genuinely hurt us is challenging. Because we struggle so much with that, we tend to do one of a few things. We bear a grudge and try anything and everything to "get back at them." We will "circle our wagons" with anyone we think will take up arms with us and then try to get even.

This is highly divisive because we involve people unaware of the conflict, creating ill feelings that were not there previously. Another thing we may do is to "put it behind us." We do not want to confront the person or deal with the drama, or the hurt is so damaging that we push it back to the farthest regions of our minds and try to forget it. Yet another thing we may do is become passive-aggressive. We pretend to be over it and force a smile when we see them, but we make snide remarks and disguise hurtful things we do to them whenever we can. But, whichever of those above you choose, you can be assured that the pain and anguish will return from time to time.

It might be when you see the person, or it may be a trigger like something told to you that will resurface the incident in your mind. When this happens, you will again feel the unforgiving hatred you carry for that person. You cannot hide hurt, you cannot ignore it, and you cannot act vengefully. It is devastating when we are vengeful, not usually to the perpetrator, but rather to us. That unforgiveness is like an anchor that weighs you down in an ocean of anger, eventually drowning all the joy out of your life. The only way to move on from someone who has sinned against you is one of the hardest things to do – forgive them.

And let's be clear: I am not saying you necessarily must restore your friendship, but I am saying that for your own sake, you should forgive them. Here is the most challenging part to hear if you have been hurt. **Mar. 11:25,** "And whenever you stand praying, forgive, if you have anything against anyone, so that your Father also who is in heaven may forgive you your trespasses." We see a similar thought given to us by the Apostle Paul in **Eph. 4:32,** "Be kind to one another, tenderhearted, forgiving one another, as God in Christ forgave you." To be forgiven, we need to forgive others. That is tough, but that is the reality of life as a Christian.

You don't have to "hang around" the perpetrator anymore, but for your own mental health and your "forever future," you need to forgive them. One last thing: forgiving someone does not mean they will not have to pay the price lawfully or spiritually if they are unrepentant, but that is not your concern. In a perfect world, the person will ask for your forgiveness and repent, but if that does not happen, you can still forgive and free yourself from the anchor.

Chapter 39
Sin and Its Domino Effect

Have you ever taken a set or more of dominoes and set them up next to each other so that you can knock one down and watch the rest fall automatically? That first one affects all the others. After they had marched around the city the required number of times, God handed Jericho into the hands of the Israelites. There was one stipulation, however. **Jos. 6:19**, "But all silver and gold, and every vessel of bronze and iron, are holy to the Lord; they shall go into the treasury of the Lord." Those items were to be devoted to the treasury of the Lord and were not for personal enrichment.

Achan did not observe the commandment, so he took some of those devoted things and hid them in his tent. This act of defiance resulted in the anger of the Lord being kindled, and He allowed them to be defeated at the hands of AI. The consequences of his treachery affected not only him but all of Israel. There are many lessons to learn from that story, but I want to concentrate on a specific one that reminds me of a set of dominoes. The moral of this particular lesson is that your sin affects more people than just you. As you fall like one of those domino pieces, you also cause others to fall.

Not only that, but the consequences can be even worse for those affected by your sins, even if you appear to escape them for the moment. For example, if you commit adultery, you may consider yourself "lucky" or "justified," but there is the genuine possibility of collateral damage you are too self-centered to notice. You deeply hurt your wife and your children. You shame your family because of your selfish, unscriptural behavior. They will have to cope with your unfaithfulness and will have to bear the mocking comments of others even though they are innocent. Not only will they be hurt, but their view of marriage may be irreparably damaged forever.

If you become addicted to drugs, those you love will suffer as well. Distress and a feeling of hopelessness will be theirs to endure as they watch you spiral out of control. Get arrested for that, or some other crime, and your loved ones will have to bear the scars and shame as well. They will be stigmatized and negatively labeled because of your sins. Pornography addiction affects those you love as well.

You will objectify women and change how you look at and treat them. They will have to suffer your sexually inappropriate comments or, worse, unhealthy attraction. There is almost no sin that does not have a domino effect of some sort, knocking down innocent people in its path and leaving chaos and destruction behind. Don't be fooled into thinking your actions are not hurting anyone else. The domino effect of sin is real.

Chapter 40

There is Joy in the Memories

Sometimes, the world seems like it has a wicked sense of humor. We rejoice one day at the birth of a child, and the very next, we mourn the loss of a loved one. At times like that, it seems we "can't win for losing," but there is always hope for the believer. In **Joh. 16:20-22** Jesus is preparing his disciples for His ascension and says the following,

> "Truly, truly, I say to you, you will weep and lament, but the world will rejoice. You will be sorrowful, but your sorrow will turn into joy. When a woman is giving birth, she has sorrow because her hour has come, but when she has delivered the baby, she no longer remembers the anguish, for joy that a human being has been born into the world." So also you have sorrow now, but I will see you again, and your hearts will rejoice, and no one will take your joy from you."

Now, I know that Jesus was speaking of his death and the subsequent victory of the resurrection, but there is much comfort to be found in those words during times of mourning. No matter the reason for the pain we are presently experiencing, a time will come when we will once again have joy. For the disciples, it was the moment they realized it was the Christ raised from the dead standing in their midst, and for us, it is the knowledge that our loved one has not been lost to us forever. Beautiful memories, hidden from our minds because of the searing pain of loss, will soon return, giving us comfort.

I love the analogy Jesus uses about the woman giving birth because the same can also be applied to us. When we lose a loved one, the anguish can be overwhelming, and life can seem cold, dark, and grim. As companionship and happiness are stolen by death, the walls of pain close in on us, shutting out the light of joy, and we can find ourselves in the dark places of hopelessness and depression. But we need to hang on to Jesus' words of hope because, in time, the sun will peek out from behind the clouds again, and we will once again feel its warmth in the shared memories of that person.

The pain of our loss should never be diminished by carelessly spoken words like "Time heals all wounds," but at the same time, we should not dig ourselves into a pit of grief we can never climb out of again. Allow yourself the time to grieve because your hour has come, but also allow yourself a time when that sense of grief turns to joy in the fond memories you have of them, the fun times you had together, the lessons you learned along the way, and above all, the love that you shared. If you are experiencing such a time of grief today, God bless you with the comfort that only He can provide, and know that you are in the prayers of those who love you.

Chapter 41

Three Words: Knowledge, Understanding, and Wisdom

"My son, if you receive my words and treasure up my commandments with you, making your ear attentive to wisdom and inclining your heart to understanding; yes, if you call out for insight and raise your voice for understanding if you seek it like silver and search for it as for hidden treasures, then you will understand the fear of the LORD and find the knowledge of God. For the LORD gives wisdom; from his mouth come knowledge and understanding" (**Pro. 2:1-6**).

When I read these six verses, three words stand out: wisdom, understanding, and knowledge. Of course, we can extrapolate much more from these verses, but I want us to focus on those three words specifically.

In what order do we receive those, and how are they related to one another? We will use the example of a pilot. Knowledge comes first and is simply a collection of information received and memorized by the individual. It comes from materials, books, and mainly from teachers' instructions. The pilot will receive information and education from class lessons and the many books he must memorize to gain the knowledge needed for his career. The dictionary defines understanding as follows; "to have the power of comprehension" or "to achieve a grasp of the nature, significance, or explanation of something."

The knowledge gained from the combination of lessons, studying, and tests gives our trainee pilot the ability to comprehend the material. In turn, this allows him to grasp the nature of flying and the dynamics that enable planes to operate in the way they do. Moreover, besides being important in his chosen career, subjects like math develop the ability to think critically and make informed decisions because he can analyze and understand a situation. In essence, it is a processing of the knowledge gained and applying it correctly. But none of the above has given him any experience yet; this is where wisdom comes into its own.

Yes, the beginning of wisdom is, to some degree, knowledge and understanding, but it is also the practical part of a pilot's training. The experience of flying and dealing with different situations and even emergencies is what we can define as wisdom. It is then "The quality of having a combination of experience, knowledge, and understanding and being able to put all of that into practice in real-world situations." For us, reading the Bible, studying it, attending Bible class, and attentively listening to sermons, among other things, is where we gain our knowledge. That allows us to understand the doctrines we have learned and apply them to our specific situations.

At the same time, wisdom is a collection of those two things with the added experience of putting all of it into practice in our lives. And, very importantly, being able to pass all that collective information and experience on to others. So, knowledge on its own is just a collection of information, and understanding comes from that knowledge. Still, it has no automatic, practical application, whereas wisdom is knowledge, understanding, and experience rolled up into one neat package. One more thing to remember: wisdom can also be gained from living life. We don't need a formal education to have wisdom; we need life experience gained in the school of hard knocks.

Chapter 42

Don't Use a Bullhorn

"Beware of practicing your righteousness before other people in order to be seen by them, for you will have no reward from your Father who is in heaven" (**Mat. 6:1**). We live in a world that desires recognition. We have awards for almost everything anyone can do, and most people strive to be "worthy" of one. Take acting as an example. There is the Emmy, the Golden Globes, the Screen Actors Guild, the Tony Award, the People's Choice Award, the Academy of Motion Arts and Sciences, and the lesser-known but very prestigious EGOT awards. The latter is for actors who have been Emmy, Grammy, Oscar, and Tony winners.

Some of these ceremonies consist of multiple categories that increase the number of awards an actor can receive. They want to be seen, want to be loved, and want to be recognized for their achievements, but often pride and arrogance are born of that desire. "Look! I did this good deed, so I need this or that recognition," they shout. The more people who see and hear of their "remarkably heroic" actions, the better they feel about themselves. They want to walk around being showered with gifts and awards and want to be honored for their "selfless" acts. If they do not receive the recognition they think they deserve, they will become hostile and resent those who did not give it to them.

The desire to receive it is like a drug that will overpower their lives, and they will scream for attention. They will do almost anything to be in line for the next "fix." These trophy hunters are so inwardly focused that they don't understand the fleeting nature of their desires. They don't realize that it does not fill the void their pride seeks to fill, and it won't last long because humans are fickle. They recognize your achievements today and may even idolize them, but soon, someone younger or more capable comes along, and they are discarded for the "next big thing."

It is no different for some Christians. Some will shout about what they have done from the rooftops to receive the accolades they think they deserve from man. The smallest act is expected to be rewarded with the most significant recognition prize. But that is not what we are told to do. **Mat. 6:2-4** reads,

"Thus, when you give to the needy, sound no trumpet before you, as the hypocrites do in the synagogues and in the streets, that they may be praised by others. Truly, I say to you, they have received their reward. But when you give to the needy, do not let your left hand know what your right hand is doing, so that your giving may be in secret. And your Father who sees in secret will reward you."

There is nothing wrong with receiving recognition for what you have done. But when it becomes the motivation for doing something, it can lead to egocentric, selfish behavior and foster an attitude of pride and arrogance. What reward of lasting value can man give you? Even if you are inducted into a "Hall of Fame," you will still receive nothing beyond this earthly realm for your achievements. Here is the key – be humble in everything you do. Do it without the need to be rewarded for your actions, and your heavenly Father will indeed reward you. Don't use a bullhorn to advertise what you have done.

Chapter 43

Are You Ashamed of the Gospel?

"For I am not ashamed of the gospel, for it is the power of God for salvation to everyone who believes, to the Jew first and also to the Greek" (**Rom. 1:16**). Anyone who knows me will tell you I have a lot of favorite verses. Almost every time I recite one, I say, "This may be one of my favorite verses." But if I were forced to choose my top ten favorites, **Rom. 1:16-17** would be among them. I have always found this a fascinating verse because of its implication. When Paul said he was not ashamed of the gospel, he had just finished saying,

> "I am under obligation to both the Greeks and the barbarians, both to the wise and to the foolish. So, I am eager to preach the gospel to you also who are in Rome." (**Rom. 1:14-15**).

Are you under the obligation to preach the gospel to everyone? Not obligated because you are being forced to, but because the drive to do so is so overwhelming that you cannot escape it. Are you eager to preach the gospel to people wherever you find yourself in this world, whether at home, in a local store, or when you are on vacation? Or are you ashamed of it? Far too many professing Christians are eager to discuss the gospel with brothers and sisters in the church but not with strangers. They debate or even argue with people on social media but do not take a moment to approach someone stumbling around in the darkness of sin.

We have much to say in church and to the few who engage us outside of it, but apart from those times, we are as silent as mice. Why is that? Why are we too afraid to share the Good News with strangers? I think we are more fearful of the persecution we may face by man than we are of answering to God. We don't like to admit it, but God seems "far away," whereas the reaction of people around us is immediate and often severe. Instead of being proud of our beliefs, we treat Jesus like a family member in jail. You love them but tend not to speak of them to anyone but family. You are ashamed to admit that you are related to them, so you avoid any conversation that could connect you to that person.

People often say, "I am just not that outgoing that I can approach strangers," or "We pay the preacher to do that. That is his job." To be clear, putting that on the preacher is a cop-out for those who are too afraid to do it themselves. The Bible clearly states that every Christian is responsible for spreading the Good News. I am sure you know people personally who are not believers, so why not talk to them? After all, someone spoke to you. Whether it was a parent, grandparent, friend, or even a stranger, someone cared enough for you to begin a conversation about Jesus with you.

Do you maybe say, "People don't want to be bothered with Christians anymore?" Are you talking about every single person in the world? I was one of those people, and it took someone more than once to ask me to go to church before I did. So, what if they ignore you or ridicule you? Who cares? Speak to enough people, and you will "close the deal," so to speak. Do you wear your Christianity like a badge of honor, or do you hide it like a family member in jail?

Chapter 44

What Kind of Mouth Do You Have?

"The mouth of the righteous is a fountain of life, but the mouth of the wicked conceals violence" (**Pro. 10:11**). Has there ever been a more accurate saying? Think of your life. I am sure there is at least one person you enjoy being around. They are positive, uplifting, and encouraging. That type of person is a pleasure to be around, and discussions are always accompanied by laughter and friendly banter. When you are having a bad day, they "reinvigorate" you, and you feel as if you can overcome whatever challenge you are facing.

That friend will never allow you to carry your burdens alone and is more than willing to pick up part or all of it to decrease your load. They are more like a brother or sister than a friend, and you look forward to spending time with this confident and upbeat friend whenever you can. There is also the opposite side of the "friendship" coin. That person is negative. They never have a good thing to say, and every discussion spirals downward into gossip and hatred for everyone and everything.

They not only see the glass half empty but usually pour out any remaining liquid until it is empty...and then throw the figurative glass at the object(s) of their hatred. The small amount of pleasure they derive from being in this world is what they get from their foul-mouthed tirades. The only connection they have to the world, the only thing that makes them feel like they have a purpose, is the negativity. They denigrate everyone and everything because it makes them feel better about themselves. Not only will they not bear your burdens with you, but they often cause the burden in the first place.

In **Jam. 3:5-8** we read about people like that, "...How great a forest is set ablaze by such a small fire...but no human being can tame the tongue...It is a restless evil, full of deadly poison..." While we all struggle to tame our tongues, these nasty people do not attempt to tame them, and they seem to derive a special kind of pleasure by speaking evil things about other people. Like the Proverb says, their mouths conceal violence because of their words. They cause all sorts of arguments and divisions but never take responsibility for their actions. Their modus operandi is always to blame someone else and then act like a victim.

They are full of hate and loathing for humanity and disrespect everyone, but then expect respect as if it is owed to them. You seldom look forward to spending time with them, and when you do, you regret it fairly quickly. By contrast, righteous people let their speech be "gracious, seasoned with salt." (**Col. 4:6**). They are kind and are always the first to encourage. They love their fellow man, are respected, and are loved because of their thoughtful speech and attitude. What kind of mouth do you have?

Chapter 45

The Dangers of Fire and Hot Coals

"Can a man carry fire next to his chest and his clothes not be burned? Of can one walk on hot coals and his feet not be scorched?" (**Pro. 6:27-28**). At first glance, it seems an obvious statement. If you carry fire near your chest, your clothes will catch fire, and walking on hot coals will definitely scorch your feet. Nevertheless, although obvious, the admonition in the form of a question is a severe warning of the dangers of negligent behavior. What could the writer possibly be speaking of that would warrant such an emphatic statement of the perils of careless actions?

The writer's intent becomes crystal clear in the very next verse. **Pro. 6:29**, "So is he who goes into his neighbor's wife; none who touches her will go unpunished." Wow! Now, the question makes perfect sense and is one many people today should hear. While the verse explicitly mentions men, it also applies to women who feed their salacious appetites. These individuals defile their marriages by trying to satisfy their lustful desires for other married men and women. This adulterous behavior will not go unpunished by God. **Heb. 13:4**, "Let marriage be held in honor among all, and let the marriage bed be undefiled, for God will judge the sexually immoral and adulterous."

I find it hard to believe how quickly people forget their marriage vows and allow their fleshly desires to corrupt their faithfulness to their spouse. Even if a single person is trying to seduce a married individual, their actions are equally dishonorable. Not only that, but their punishment for defiling the marriage bed will be just as severe. The problem is that we live in a world where the only thing that matters is us. We don't care about the consequences of our actions and will try to justify them with some weak excuse – as long as we can satisfy our licentious cravings.

The world will applaud us for "putting us first" and will gladly stand by and watch yet another marriage spiral into distrust and hatred, only to end in divorce. The writer wants us to understand the severity of actions that cause disharmony in a marriage and thus uses fire to emphasize the point. We all have an innate fear of being burned, and most of us will do anything to prevent that kind of searing pain. Interestingly, he uses fire for another reason: it reminds us of sin's eternal consequences. Maybe it should serve as a wake-up call for those thinking of doing something like that or already are.

It is not too late to stop acting so sinfully and repent. God is merciful and will forgive you if you genuinely mean it and give up the sin. We all make mistakes or even purposely act in ways contrary to the teachings of God, but unless we die in that sin, we can and will be forgiven. It only takes the realization that we are on a path to certain doom and the determination to cast aside the sin that is like fire next to our chest or the hot coals under our feet.

Chapter 46
What Are You a Reflection Of?

"...For the Lord sees not as man sees: man looks on the outward appearance, but the Lord looks on the heart" (1Sa. 16:7). "As a counselor, more than one teen has come up to me in the past and complained about how people viewed them. Maybe they were not good-looking enough, not sporty enough, or simply not cool enough to satisfy the egocentric nature of a group of ignorant people in their school. After hearing them speak, I would point to a saying I had written on a whiteboard in my office, "I am who I AM says I am." This is not something you will find in the Bible, but it is an important one that absolutely has its foundations in the Good Book.

We live in a world where the popular media decides what "cool" is. It determines what weight we should be, the shape of our bodies, what we should wear and how we should act, etc. It is also a world where those who do not meet prescribed standards are judged as if they designed themselves and made some huge mistake. "You are so ugly!", "How can you live with yourself, fatty?" "You are as dumb as a rock, you idiot!" "If I were as ugly as you, I would kill myself!" and "You are just a monkey!" are only some of the disparaging things they are forced to hear daily. Well, let me tell you something today, "GOD DOES NOT MAKE MISTAKES."

God designed you with intent. He did not look at a fake, photoshopped model in "Vogue" magazine as the blueprint for what you should look like. He did not take the sculpting knife and begin to shape you into that model, only to be distracted by a squirrel in the yard and slip up. He did not look at you and say, "Oh, My, that was a mistake, but I am running behind and will have to let this one go as is." Unlike the world, God will not place those considered beautiful before you in Heaven. There will not be a group of "cool" kids and then the "rest." He will not discriminate based on your imperfections because your outward appearance is of no heavenly value. You are a beautiful creature created by a perfect God.

Please don't listen to the ignorance of those who attack you for not looking like them. They are the insecure, selfish ones who need self-affirmation to make themselves feel relevant and important. Usually, they are hiding some pain, some deep, dark secret, and the only way they can cope is to belittle other people. Pity them even as they denigrate you because they are way sadder than you are. You are not the ugly one; they are. Stand up, keep your head high, and walk in the confidence of knowing that God made every inch of you just the way He wanted.

And I bet you anything, when He finished, He stood back and was incredibly proud of you. Why? Because your personality, your humility and respect for others, your patience and kindness, your tolerance, and your love for humanity – even those who insult you – reflect what He desires. When you are attacked, don't be ashamed; be proud because you are a child of God, not man. Unlike those deluded souls, you are heaven-bound.

Chapter 47

Your Request Has Been Denied

"You ask and do not receive, because you ask wrongly, to spend it on your passions" (**Jam. 4:3**). Many people become angry because they ask for something in prayer but do not receive it. They will quote scriptures like **Mar. 11:24**, "Therefore I tell you, whatever you ask for in prayer, believe that you have received it and it will be yours." Why would God dismiss their requests? Why do other people who are not even Christians receive "tons" of good things, and they, His children, receive nothing? They begin to stumble in their faith and even begin to deny His ability to answer prayers.

Some even deny His existence altogether, as if he could only prove it by answering their every request. What they fail to realize is that God has an intimate knowledge of their motivations and will decide based on that whether to answer a specific prayer or not. Ignoring for a second the debate as to whether Christians should play the lottery or not, some religiously play it every chance they can in the hopes of winning. Before handing over their hard-earned money, they pray to win so that they can use the proceeds to "bless others." While that sounds noble enough, history has shown that most people do not do so after winning.

A tiny portion may, in some cases, be handed to a local church or charity, but the vast majority is spent on their passions. They may pray for God to bless them with a person they "love," and then, if their prayer is answered, their lascivious desires overtake them, and they live in sin. Most of these unspiritual passions will do nothing to increase their faith and commitment to the Lord but instead drive them away from service to His kingdom. Many people fail to understand God's foreknowledge in all matters. He knows what is best for us long before we do, and we usually only recognize that in hindsight. God wants to shower us with blessings, but like a wise parent, He knows what will lead us to ruin and what will benefit us.

So, it is essential to remember **1Jo. 5:14** when praying, "And this is the confidence that we have toward him, that if we ask anything according to his will, he hears us." The easy part is to do what we all do – pray for what we want instead of what we need. The hard part is giving it to God and then accepting His will for our lives. If we pray for selfish reasons, even when they are cleverly disguised as having charitable motivations, our prayers will be heard but not answered. Even when we are praying for someone else, and our intentions are honorable and selfless, the Lord may have another outcome in mind, and it is then that our faith in God is truly tested. Since we have no knowledge or understanding of the future, we need to place our faith in God and trust His ability to do what is best overall. The key to successful prayer is **Pro. 3:5**, "Trust in the Lord with all your heart, and do not lean on your own understanding."

Chapter 48

The Dangers of Uncontrolled Anger

"Know this, my beloved brothers: let every person be quick to hear, slow to speak, slow to anger; for the anger of man does not produce the righteousness of God" (**Jam. 1:19-20**).

Are you angry? Most people have a degree of anger, even if it is buried deep within them. Under the right circumstances, that rage will seek to find its way to the surface and erupt like lava from a dormant volcano. Many people can subdue their anger. However, some either cannot or choose not to. Suddenly and without warning, like the pyroclastic clouds of an erupting volcano, their anger bursts forth to consume everything in its path.

Its destructive nature will give rise to actions that cannot be undone. A spouse, child, friend, or stranger will become the victim of that fury, and hurtful things will be said or done. In traffic, it can lead to "road rage" with terrible consequences at times as the vehicle is used as a weapon. This kind of anger is manifested at sporting events where parents attack the referee or other parents. The tragedies emanating from this kind of vicious behavior have led to the loss of friends, spousal and child abuse, divorce, loss of jobs, criminal charges, and even fatalities. Seemingly timid men and women can instantly be transformed into monsters that ravenously feed off the fear and pain of their victims.

Not even their most sincere apology will curb their paroxysm of rage because the same fury that released the monster will trample their sense of empathy and understanding for their victim. Even more sad is the fact that rage acts like a forest fire; once started, it consumes more and more and becomes ever more challenging to control, leaving destruction, grief, and even death in its wake. Anger like that does not hear, does not reason, does not empathize, and does not forgive.

Violence is its only weapon, and vengeance is its only goal. It descends into madness with less and less need for provocation as a false but enabling sense of power rises from every such event. At first, their outbursts are followed by sincere regret and guilt, but as with the lessening need for provocation, these emotions diminish and vanish over time. They use excuses like, "Your actions forced me," "I was only retaliating to protect myself," or "I blacked out and lost control." They may even point to Jesus's anger in the temple and call their actions "righteous," but ultimately, all they are trying to do is excuse their inability to control their emotions.

Most of us can curb our anger, even if we get to the point of saying hurtful things we do not mean. Obviously, some choose not to. These are the people that James is warning to slow down and listen before acting on their emotions. Listening is the best defuser of anger in the world because it often negates the need to be angry in the first place. When you understand the other person's actions or intentions, you may realize it was not meant to be provocative and thus remain calm and in control.

Chapter 49

Don't Give the Enemy a Weapon and Ammunition

"So faith comes from hearing, and hearing through the word of Christ" (**Rom. 10:17**). If there ever has been a saying that irritates me, it is "Faith is blind!" Some people use that as the foundation for their faith in God, and I understand what they are trying to convey. God is indeed transcendent and visually invisible as a physical entity. We cannot see and touch Him, so they tell unbelievers who question their faith that they do not need to prove everything they believe. In their quest to explain what they mean, they quote **Heb. 11:1**, "Now faith is the assurance of things hoped for, the conviction of things not seen."

I have even heard people say that faith in God is like love. We know it exists because we feel it, but we cannot see or even describe it entirely – it just is. "Faith is blind" is a dangerous argument because it allows attackers of the Christian faith to use that very saying against us. The atheist Christopher Hitchens once wrote, "Faith is the surrender of the mind; it's the surrender of reason, it's the surrender of the only (thing) that that makes us different from other mammals." Saying our faith is blind is handing a weapon and ammunition to the enemy of God's Word and then being forced to defend what we believe.

Possibly the most famous of all modern-day atheists, Richard Dawkins, had this to say about faith, "Faith is the great cop-out, the great excuse to evade the need to think and evaluate evidence. Faith is belief despite, even perhaps because of, the lack of evidence." Once again, you can see the danger of telling opponents of the Christian faith that we have no evidence for what we believe. When we relegate our beliefs to a subjective understanding of something we have no proof of, we are automatically in defense mode, and that is a dangerous place to be. While defending our faith is just and noble, saying it is blind is inaccurate.

Our faith is not a blind, emotional response to a desire for a belief in something greater than ourselves. God Himself might be invisible, but that does not mean we do not have overwhelming evidence to prove His existence and, subsequently, our faith. **Rom. 1:17** dispels that incorrect assumption by confirming that our faith comes to us from hearing the words of scripture. All the evidence we need is in the Good Book. **Rom. 1:20** reads as follows,

> "For his invisible attributes, namely, his eternal power and divine nature, have been clearly perceived, ever since the creation of the world, in the things that have been made. So they are without excuse."

He may be invisible, but His attributes and evidence for His existence are not – it is in the complexities of life, the position of the sun and the moon, the moral standard derived from His Word, and countless other things. Thus, **Heb. 11:1** is the assurance that the conviction exists despite Him being physically invisible. But that verse does not claim that faith is blind. Almost daily, new archaeological evidence confirms what was once considered a myth. Moreover, the Bible contains many facts that indisputably prove the reliability of scripture and, thus, the existence of God. Your faith is not blind if you look for evidence.

Chapter 50
Stop Watering Dead Plants

"And after some days Paul said to Barnabas, 'Let us return and visit the brothers in every city where we proclaimed the word of the Lord, and see how they are.' Now Barnabas wanted to take with them John called Mark. But Paul thought best not to take with them one who had withdrawn from them in Pamphylia and had not gone with them to the work. And there arose a sharp disagreement, so that they separated from each other..." (**Act. 15:36-39**).

Paul and Barnabas were friends. Both were loyal followers of Christ but did not see eye to eye.

I quoted those verses to say, "It is okay to disagree, and it is okay sometimes to realize that a friendship may be better off if each person went their separate directions." If you have had a friend, even briefly, you know that arguments are inevitable. Those people we call "best friends" usually earn that title because we have successfully weathered the storms of life together. And some of those storms are within the friendship. We do not always agree, but how we act during the disagreement, especially afterward, reflects our commitment to the friendship. I can never understand why some Christian friendships dissolve so easily.

I am not saying that every friendship should be lifelong, but that some end for no good reason. We all know we say and do stupid things during an argument, so why be so unforgiving? Why allow your small ego or pride to stand in the way of continuing those friendships? You may not be "besties" anymore, but how can you act that way and still call yourself a Christian? That said, there are certain friendships that should end altogether.

I may sound like I am contradicting my last statement, but hear me out. I came across a brilliant saying recently; "Stop watering dead plants!" In other words, don't spend energy on friendships that are all but dead anyway. These friendships may have had value in the past, but they have had their season. That does not mean you have to be mean about how you end it, but it does mean that it is okay to do so. You can calmly and respectfully move on from them. Go your separate ways and find other friendships that add value to your life.

There is also the type of friendship that falls on bad times. This is the type of friendship Paul and Barnabas had. I am confident that Paul and Barnabas did not let the "sharp disagreement" end their mutual respect or friendship. It is safe to assume that a heated conversation must have occurred before they went their separate ways, which was okay. Our life paths may force friendships to veer off in different directions for a time, but we should not "burn those bridges" because one day, we might share the same path again. If we summarily end the relationship because of temporary differences, there might be no opportunity to reconcile it anymore. Be smart if you decide to part ways. Be Christian about it. Make sure the plant is totally dead before you stop watering it.

Chapter 51
Just Do It

Paul loved the people of God, and there are many examples of him praising both congregations and individuals. In **Rom. 1:8**, he expresses his thankfulness for them, "First, I thank God through Jesus Christ for all of you, because your faith is proclaimed in all the world." Paul also says the following to the Ephesian church,

> "For this reason, because I have heard of your faith in the Lord Jesus and your love toward all the saints, I do not cease to give thanks for you, remembering you in my prayers." (**Eph. 1:15-16**).

Not only did he pray for the Ephesian church, but he frequently mentions the same practice for other churches;

> "For God is my witness, whom I serve with my spirit in the gospel of his Son, that without ceasing I mention you always in my prayers, asking that somehow by God's will I may now at last succeed in coming to you." (**Rom. 1:9-10**).

Paul cared for other Christians, and so should we. As an associate minister in Dallas, Texas, I visited members of the congregation, and I was always welcomed with joy. I also developed deep and lasting friendships with those who visited with me.

Todd, a special "fellow visitor," and I both enjoyed the opportunity to spend a few minutes in fellowship with various members of the church we attended. We derived immense pleasure from sitting and chatting with people in their homes, and our friendship also grew stronger with each visit. We made a great team because we would "insult" each other, calling ourselves the visitor's "favorite" and generally making the experience light-hearted. Of course, there were times when the visits were more serious, and friendly banter was shelved for a while, but we also enjoyed those moments.

Todd was the main fellow visitor but not the only one. His wife, Elaine, our friends Cathy, Sharon, and Albert, and my wife, Melinda, would be among others who would accompany us from time to time. We were a happy group because our visits brought happiness to so many people. We would pray for people, laugh with them, grieve with them, and, without exception, grow closer to them. We even visited some for their last moments on this earth – a privilege that cannot be overstated.

If you can, visit a few members and see how quickly endearing friendships are formed. The encouragement from visiting is mutual, and getting to know each other more personally is a beautiful and uplifting experience. Paul thought so much of it that he even called visiting "pure religion" in **Jam. 1:27**, "Pure religion and undefiled before God and Father is this, to visit the fatherless and widows in their affliction...," And remember this, you may be the only visitor they receive. So, to quote a famous sports brand logo, "Just do it."

Chapter 52

You May Find Yourself in a Cold, Dark Place

"Many are the plans in the mind of a man, but it is the purpose of the Lord that will stand" (**Pro. 19:21**). Most people are so quick to make their own plans that they forget the purpose of the Lord for their lives. They are influenced by their parents, friends, or peers and "go it alone." The problem is that when we ignore the will of the Lord for our lives, we risk coming to ruin. How many of us have dived headlong into this or that and then lived to regret it? Should we plan things ourselves? Of course, God will not email you a set of instructions to follow, but that does not mean you should not take His will into account.

As a young Bible student, I asked a lecturer how I would know if I was about to do my will or God's. I will never forget his response. "If it is easy, it is probably your choice. Carefully consider the more difficult choice because you may see God's purpose in that one. He will challenge you more than you will." We should pray to God and ask Him to provide the answer to us, and then we should be willing to follow it, even if it seems the more difficult choice. God's most precious gifts are the ones that are the most challenging to open. You may struggle to untie it or unwrap it. You may get a paper cut along the way, but the prize will be worth every bit of struggle.

The Almighty sees so much that we do not, and He can steer us away from paths that will ultimately not be in our best interests. **Pro. 3:5** says, "Trust in the Lord with all of your heart," but we have a problem doing that when personal desires like comfort, finances, location, and status lead our thoughts. Ultimately, the purpose of the Lord will stand, but the road to that is often paved with obstacles of our own making. We try "our" way and fight the will of the Lord, only to discover in hindsight that listening to Him the first time would have prevented much hardship.

Look at the example of Jonah. He would not listen to God. He even tried to run away, but where did that get him? Overboard and in the belly of a sea creature. Refusing to listen to God will not work out any better for you because you will find yourself in a cold, dark place. Then, the only voice you will hear will be His. And, maybe then you will listen. Pray that God will open the right doors. Believe in your heart that He is the Lord of your life, and you will find your path is made straight. That does not mean there will be no obstacles, but straight because when we follow the purpose of the Lord in our lives, our victory is assured.

Jeremiah was a young man who had to deliver his message to the Israelite exiles in Babylon. In a letter, he assures them with the following words of God,

> "For I know the plans I have for you, declares the Lord, plans for welfare and not for evil, to give you a future and a hope. Then you will call upon me and come and pray to me, and I will hear you." (**Jer. 29:11-12**).

God has a plan for your life. If you take the time to discern what His will is for your life, you will have a future and a hope. But to grab onto that, you need to call out to Him in prayer.

Chapter 53

Do You Preach Love but Practice Hatred?

"...You shall love the Lord your God with all your heart and with all your soul and with all your mind. This is the great and first commandment. And a second is like it: You shall love your neighbor as yourself" (**Mat. 22:37-39**).

Do you love your neighbor as yourself? Most people would have no difficulty understanding the words of Jesus. They were not given to us using a parable, and we do not need some detailed study of the etymology (origin) of the words to decipher them. We are to love God first and foremost, and then we are to love our fellow man, as well. We should love them as much as we love ourselves.

One would think something so clear and concise would be relatively simple to implement, so why do some people have so much difficulty with it? Folks sit in church every week or, if they do not attend regularly, read their Bibles and pray daily. They hear sermons on loving each other and other such commands, but when it comes to practicing what they have heard or read, they fail miserably. This is not an indictment of every person in the church, but as a minister and a counselor, I have encountered this more times than I ever thought I would have.

On another occasion, a gentleman came up to me with money for the youth in his hand. We were on the way to take them to summer camp and really appreciated the gesture – until he put a condition on giving it. He looked at me and then pointed to two of the kids. "Are those two dating?" he asked. "No, I replied, they are just good friends." "Good!" he said, handing me the money. I refused to take it. I am sure every one of us has similar stories to recount, but do we stand up to individuals when they act that way? There is a show on a local television station called "What Would You Do?" They place actors in different scenarios and then use hidden cameras to see if members of the public will intervene to correct the situation.

If you have seen one of those episodes, I bet you had a big smile on your face when some brave soul stood up for the "victim," but would you do the same? Are you someone who attacks or someone who intervenes for the sake of justice? That would probably be a good time to think about the WWJD acronym, "What would Jesus do?" What would you do? Do you preach love but practice hatred? If you do, what would it take to make you understand that your actions are heinous? Does the very real and deserving threat of an eternity in hell not deter you from acting hatefully toward others? And if you are one of many Christians who love your neighbor as yourself, thank you.

You are an encouragement, and your actions do not go unnoticed. Your love for others is the primary factor that will turn the corrupt heart of a hateful person into a loving, kind, and considerate one. Work with them. Admonish them in love, pray for them, and study the Bible together. That way, they can learn and understand that we are all the same in the eyes of Christ. **Gal. 3:28**, "There is neither Jew nor Greek, there is neither slave nor free, there is no male and female, for you are all one in Christ Jesus."

Chapter 54

Chase Wisdom and Christianity, Not Money

"He who loves money will not be satisfied with money, nor he who loves wealth with his income" (**Ecc. 5:10**). Many people think that money will solve all their problems, but that is not the case. I know a millionaire who always says that with more money comes more problems, and I believe that. There is also the issue of "for-money-friends." Those are the fair-weather type of friends who will surround you like a pack of hungry hyenas. They will gladly help you spend your money until it is exhausted before deserting you faster than you can say "parasite."

Rich people are not always happy. Their marriages aren't always secure. Their children don't necessarily act better. Suicide still occurs. And yet, because they have never experienced riches, many think that life as a wealthy person automatically includes peace and happiness. They play the lottery religiously each week and even go to casinos to gamble money they do not have, hoping to hear the familiar sound of a machine hitting the jackpot. They will also hop from one job to another for one or two more dollars per hour if they think it will get them closer to their goal of "financial independence."

The problem is that financial independence is a fluid concept that moves in relation to money earned, so it is an elusive goal regardless of your bank account size. I say that because the more you make, the more expensive your tastes become. Win the lottery, and you will not be satisfied with your present living conditions. No longer will you stay in your tiny house and drive your used vehicle with 100,000 miles on it. You will find a much bigger home and a fancy car to match your new wealth. Your clothes will cost more; you will buy expensive everything and dine in the best restaurants. You will quickly find those leeches who become your new best friends as you throw the "poor" old ones to the curb.

The result will be the same financial pinch you are in now, relatively speaking. You will continue to seek more wealth to achieve that ever-elusive financial independence. Just as **Eccl. 5:10** states: you will never be satisfied with your wealth. Happiness cannot be found in banknotes. I am not saying to be poor and never to try to better yourself financially, and neither does the Bible teach that. Solomon was a man of God and one of the wealthiest people who has ever lived, so wealth per se is not the enemy. The true enemy is your attitude toward it. That is clearly seen in **1 Ti. 6:10,**

> "For the love of money is a root of all kinds of evils. It is through this craving that some have wandered away from the faith and pierced themselves with many pangs."

The message is that you should not seek riches to the exclusion of your family and other relationships and, more importantly, your spirituality. Happiness is found in contentment and spiritual commitment, as witnessed in **Heb. 13:5,** "Keep your life free from the love of money and be content with what you have." Don't chase money: chase wisdom and Christianity instead.

Chapter 55

Fear Destroys Hope

"O LORD, make me know my end and what is the measure of my days; let me know how fleeting I am! Behold, you have made my days a few handbreadths, and my lifetime is as nothing before you. Surely, all humanity stands as a mere breath! Selah. Surely a man goes about as a shadow! Surely for nothing, they are in turmoil; man heaps up wealth and does not know who will gather!" (**Psa. 39:4-6**).

The writer of this Psalm has had much difficulty in his life. He bridled his tongue, remaining silent even during all that he was going through, but he says that did not help because his "distress grew worse" (**v.3**).

Now he beseeches the Lord to allow him to know how long he will have to suffer on this earth before death brings an escape from all his hardships. Most people have suffered enough that they may have been tempted to or did ask that question at least at one point in their lives. Even though death is a great fear of man, there are times when it appears to offer respite enough to make us look forward to it. The author also wants to understand his frailty in this regard, but it is important to note that he is not asking for the exact knowledge about his end, something we are never promised in the scriptures.

It is not for us to know that, as we are clearly told in **Jam. 4:14**, "Yet you do not know what tomorrow will bring. What is your life? For you are a mist that appears for a little time and then vanishes." It is comforting to know that our suffering will not continue forever. What is important to know is not how long we will live but, as we see in the next verse, the understanding of the power of God. It is He who made us. **Isa. 64:8** reads, "But now, O Lord, You are our Father. We are the clay, and You are the potter." It stands to reason that our creator, the one who breathed life into us, who created us to dwell on this earth for a few "handbreadths" of time, controls all things.

It also means that He can deliver on His promise of a glorious afterlife free from the struggles and pains of this one. The writer can find solace in the fact that the Almighty has him in mind and will never leave or forsake him even during the darkest times, and so should we. Our focus should not be on this life but on the one to come. The writer warns of placing all of one's efforts on things of this earth when he says, "Man heaps up wealth and does not know who will gather!" If we concentrate on the things of this life, it is easy to lose focus on the things of the next.

Then, our trials become overwhelming because we lose sight of the power of God to help us overcome life's difficulties. Focus on God, and there is hope irrespective of our present circumstances. Losing sight of God and fear controls the present, which can devastate our psyche because it destroys hope. So, focus on God and the future and ask Him for patience and perseverance to cope with and overcome your present difficulties.

Chapter 56

Are You a Gossip?

Occasionally, I get asked something that should be relatively straightforward but isn't. Almost all of us are guilty of it occasionally, while others are guilty of it all the time. I am referring to gossip and the confusion that seems to surround it. Two questions seem to dominate the conversation. When is talking to someone gossiping? And is it a sin? Merriam-Webster defines it as "a person who habitually reveals personal or sensational facts about others." Dictionary.com defines it as "idle talk or rumor, especially about the personal or private affairs of others." In contrast, the Cambridge Dictionary defines it as "conversation or reports about other people's private lives that might be unkind, disapproving, or not true."

The first thing you will notice from the above is how broad the definition is. First, look at the second question: "Is it a sin?" The Bible is clearly against gossiping, as we read in **Rom. 1:29-31**, where it is among multiple sins listed,

> "They were filled with all manner of unrighteousness, evil, covetousness, malice. They are full of envy, murder, strife, deceit, and maliciousness. They are gossips, slanderers, haters of God, insolent, haughty, boastful, inventors of evil, disobedient to parents, foolish, faithless, heartless, ruthless...."

Gossip slanders a person's character, and when the purpose is to do that, it comes from a bad person and is a sin. **Pro. 11:13**, "Whoever goes about slandering reveals secrets, but he who is trustworthy in spirit keeps a thing covered."

Loosely defining it makes us all guilty of it all the time. Is venting to a spouse or friend gossip? Are we guilty of doing so when stating facts about an incident or event? Usually, we would quickly define anything said about us as gossip, but when we discuss other people, we define it as a "confidential conversation." How can we prevent ourselves from doing it if we do not know its proper definition? Gossip has a negative spirit attached to it. A conversation where you defend yourself against the actions of others using facts is not gossip.

Venting to a friend isn't either if it is not explicitly meant to hurt the feelings or reputation of another. Asking someone for advice by stating the facts of an incident is also not gossip.

Clearly, there has to be some ill intention involved, usually coupled with exaggeration or outright lies. Being a busybody about the affairs of others is gossiping. Habitually speaking of others negatively by slandering them is also. A Greek definition of this was given to me in university. It defined gossip as "a discussion that is derogatory about someone shared in confidence with others that is not motivated by doing good or in personal defense and is accompanied by an enjoyment in hurting that person." I like that definition, but one word of caution – there is a fine line between discussion and gossip, so be careful what you say. Also, when you repeat what is said to you in confidence, gossip is likely what you are engaging in, especially when a sensational element motivates the conversation.

To ensure you do not fall into the trap of gossiping, use **Eph. 4:29** as a reliable indicator for not crossing the line, "Let no corrupting talk come out of your mouths, but only such as is good for building up, as fits the occasion, that it may give grace to those who hear."

Chapter 57

Are You a Peter?

How do you act when you are not in church or not among your Christian friends? Do you wear your Christianity like a badge of honor for people to see, or do you store that badge in the drawer next to the dusty Bible until you go to church services on Sunday morning? In **Mat. 26:69-75**, Peter denies Christ three times, even doing so with an oath, swearing he did not know the Savior. As most people already know, the rooster then crows, and Peter remembers the words of Jesus, "Before the rooster crows, you will deny Me three times." I imagine that was not one of his favorite moments, and I am pretty sure he felt the shame of his denial.

Unfortunately, that practice is more common than you may think among professing believers. If we go to services every Sunday and profess his glory in the company of other Christians but then live like heathens when they are not around, we are, in essence, denying Him. We cannot have one foot in the church's door and the other in the world. We cannot live two lives separate from each other as we try to please God on the one hand and the world on the other. In fact, we are warned of that very attitude in **Jam. 4:4**,

> "You adulterous people! Do you not know that friendship with the world is enmity with God? Therefore, whoever wishes to be a friend of the world makes himself an enemy of God."

When you put Christ on in baptism, you must put off the things of the world. You cannot decide when you will not be faithful to Christ. The problem is that the deceptive allure of the fleeting recognition of the world traps many Christians in an unfaithful relationship with Christ. We then end up cheating on Him in the same way an adulterer cheats on their spouse. Of course, we all know the danger of explicitly denying Christ because it is clearly articulated in scriptures like **Mat. 10:33**, "But whoever denies Me before men, I will also deny before My Father who is in heaven." The end of anyone who is not faithful is eternal separation from God, resulting in everlasting agony in hell.

But we should not be fooled into thinking that verbalizing it is the only way to deny Him. The saying "actions speak louder than words" is an excellent example of this because it is also by our actions that we confess or deny our Lord and Savior. Deciding to follow God through Christ our Lord is always our choice, but once we choose to do so and put Christ on in baptism, we do not have the option to live double lives. That choice remains ours to make, but the consequences of doing so are dire, and we ought to think carefully before committing to Christ if we are only going to be half-hearted about it.

In **Rev. 3:15-16**, we read the following words,

> "I know your works: you are neither cold nor hot. Would that you were either cold or hot! So, because you are lukewarm, and neither hot nor cold, I will spit you out of my mouth."

These words of warning clearly illustrate the dangers of denying Christ by our actions. Can you confidently say that your actions are evidence of your faith, or are you a Peter, denying Christ for fear of what the world will think or do to you?

Chapter 58

Are the "Last Days" Far Off?

"But understand this, that in the last days there will come times of difficulty. For people will be lovers of self, lovers of money, proud, arrogant, abusive, disobedient to their parents, ungrateful, unholy, heartless, unappeasable, slanderous, without self-control, brutal, not loving good, treacherous, reckless, swollen with conceit, lovers of pleasure rather than lovers of God, having the appearance of godliness, but denying its power. Avoid such people" (**2Ti. 3:1-5**).

The first question to ask here is when the "last days" are. For many, it is some time in the distant future, so they do not feel a sense of accountability and responsibility for the present. Not that it means the ability to sin without consequence exists, but for many people, the "last days" would be a time to start paying particular attention to God and His commands. Think about a time in school when you were given an assignment. Except for a tiny minority, the average student would wait for more than half the allowed time to elapse before beginning to work on it. Some would even wait until the proverbial last second before starting, but all would take the project progressively more seriously as the final day grew closer.

Let's consider when we should take spiritual matters in the abovementioned verses more seriously. **Heb. 1:1-2** reads, "Long ago, at many times and in many ways, God spoke to our fathers through the prophets, but in these "LAST DAYS" He has spoken to us by His son...." Clearly, the last days started with Jesus and are not sometime in the distant future. However, there is a difference between knowing it is the last days and trying to predict the end times. The "last days" is an undetermined period that began with Jesus and, therefore, cannot be used to defend an "end-time prophesy."

The scriptures clearly indicate that we have no indication of the latter, as seen in **1Th. 5:1-2**,

"Now concerning the times and the seasons, brothers, you have no need to have anything written to you. For you yourselves are fully aware that the day of the Lord will come like a thief in the night."

But that does not mean we should not take the words seriously because the day we will answer for what we have done may not be far away. Each of us has, on average, 78.8 years before we face the music, so to speak. Some have less, and some more, but more or less, we are essentially in the end times because of our limited lifespan. This is especially true since that day is a surprise that could come at any time. Take the warnings seriously.

Chapter 59
Garrulous Speech

"If anyone thinks he is religious and does not bridle his tongue but deceives his heart, this person's religion is worthless" (**Jam. 1:26**). What a warning James issues for his readers. If you know me, you know that I talk a lot, so scriptures that speak to that topic really affect me. I have had people in the past approach me to say that the Bible clearly says we "talkers" should bridle our tongues. At least one person told me they "fear" for my salvation because of my tendency to "converse too freely." I have also been approached by fellow concerned "talkers" who feel at risk because of that tendency.

People who talk a lot carry their thoughts in their own words, so we must be careful to express what we are processing before it is complete in our minds. Obviously, this can cause problems because the wrong message may be relayed before the proper one is formulated. Therefore, the tendency to misspeak, albeit unintentionally, is real. Talkers also tend to babble on and on, not making sense because they want to be heard all the time.

The Bible warns about that kind of speech in verses like **Pro. 10:8**, "The wise of heart will receive commandments, but a babbling fool will come to ruin," and **Ecc. 5:2-3**,

> "Be not rash with your mouth, nor let your heart be hasty to utter a word before God, for God is in heaven, and you are on earth. Therefore, let your words be few. For a dream comes with much business and a fool's voice with many words."

Every person should be careful not to be compelled to give utterances to every thought that pops into the head instead of carefully choosing the appropriate words.

Moreover, suppose you are garrulous (chatty, especially about trivial matters). In that case, you need to pay special attention to listening instead of interrupting and talking all the time. **Jam. 1:19** speaks to that with these words, "Know this, my beloved brothers: let every person be quick to hear...." Take the time to hear what the other person has to say before inserting volumes of hastily spewed-out words to be heard. Okay, so the Bible clearly states that we should choose our words carefully, but I would warn you not to hastily gossip about those rather talkative people.

If you speak behind the backs of talkative people, you may want to read verses like **Pro. 16:28**. Should you then refrain from helping someone who is chatty from being a babbler? Absolutely not, but first, understand the distinction between wordy and garrulous. And, if you have a reputation for verbosity, ensure that what comes out is well thought out and used for constructive encouragement instead of babbling words.

Chapter 60
We Do Not See, and Yet We Believe

"Though you have not seen him, you love him. Though you do not now see him, you believe in him and rejoice with joy that is inexpressible and filled with glory, obtaining the outcome of your faith, the salvation of your souls" (**1Pe. 1:8-9**).

In a preceding verse (**v. 7**), we read, "...may be found to result in praise and glory and honor at the revelation of Jesus Christ." With these words, Peter celebrates the fact that his readers, Christians scattered across northern Asia, were loyal and loved Christ even though they had not witnessed Christ personally.

Unlike them, Peter had been among the privileged to be present with Christ – **Act. 10:41**, "...not to all the people but to us who had been chosen by God as witnesses, who ate and drank with Him after He rose from the dead." We can sense the admiration Peter expressed with those words while perhaps remembering the words of Jesus to "doubting" Thomas. Thomas would not believe Christ rose without proof, so Jesus appeared before the disciples and told Thomas to "Put your fingers here, and see My hands, and put your hand, and place it in My side."

The words Peter undoubtedly remembered later, then followed, "Have you believed because you have seen Me? Blessed are those who have not seen and yet have believed." (**Joh. 20:29**) and **v. 27**, Do not disbelieve but believe." How much more does that apply to you and me? We are not a few years removed from the life of Christ on earth, but millennia, and yet we still believe. We don't require physical proof of our faith in Christ because we understand and believe **Heb. 11:1**, "Now faith is the assurance of things hoped for, the conviction of things not seen."

But it is more than the conviction of things not seen because we have read the words of **Rom. 1:20** and have experienced them for ourselves –

"For his invisible attributes, namely, his eternal power and divine nature, have been clearly perceived, ever since the creation of the world, in the things that have been made. So they are without excuse."

We understand that the beautiful things of this earth bear witness to the existence of God. We accept that reality not because we are "blind" but precisely because we are not. While we don't need tangible proof, we are lucky enough to have been given that concerning the Bible in the form of manuscripts and parts of manuscripts.

Ours is a faith that is experienced in the reality of physical evidence and the existence of that which cannot be touched but is still evidenced in our hearts and minds. Knowing that we have a beautiful destiny beyond our understanding, as promised in **1Co. 2:9** increases our faith exponentially and is genuinely motivating. And being aware of and believing that promise is a prize too grand for most of us to let go of. So, we, the blessed who have not seen and yet believe, live our lives in thankful gratitude to the work of Christ on the cross for each one of us.

Chapter 61

Wrongfully Pursuing Our Desires (Pt.1)

"It happened, late one afternoon when David arose from his couch and was walking on the roof of the king's house, that he saw from the roof a woman bathing; and the woman was very beautiful" (**2Sa. 11:2**).

2 Samuel 11 and 12 should serve as a warning. When we desire something, we often overlook important facts and pursue it without considering the consequences.

I think it's entirely plausible to assume the king did not initially know the woman he was looking at was married. Either he did not ask or simply did not care to know as he used his considerable power to obtain his heart's desire. We can act similarly. We may not have a king's power, but we have many tools to achieve our goal. To conquer our victim, we use whatever influence we have, like a position of authority, age, smooth-talking, lying, manipulation, looks, or even blackmail. And make no mistake about it: Bathsheba was a victim.

Any desire we have that we know or come to know is an outright sin becomes our Bathsheba. Yes, we may not initially realize the desire is wrong, but what happens when we do? Very often, the fact that it is wrong does not deter us from achieving our goal. We justify it with some lie like "If she were not bathing in plain sight or did not so readily give into my advances, I would have stopped," but would we have? If it is about material possessions, we justify it by saying, "It will not hurt anyone." If it is an addiction, we say, "I can keep it under control," or "I can stop whenever I want." But that is seldom the case. Sometimes, we simply don't care if we get what we want. The fact is that desire can be a powerful drug. We sweep any guilt under the rug and dive headlong into our "drug of choice," reveling in the fleeting satisfaction it brings, but that won't last long.

David got what he wanted, but then things "went south." Sometimes, we get what we want, but then reality catches up with us, and we must make alternate plans to extricate ourselves from the situation. As you will no doubt remember from the story of David and Bathsheba in 2Sa. 11 and 12, the king immediately hashes a diabolical plan to save himself by inviting her husband home from the battlefield to spend the night with her. You see, she is pregnant, and David wants to flee the situation instead of taking responsibility for his actions.

We do the same when we try to blame someone else for our mistakes in life. Almost anything seems better than the truth, so we concoct some devious plan, but, as with David, it never works out quite as planned. Since Uriah does not want to desert his soldiers, the plan does not work, and David decides to entertain him and make him drunk. The king is sure that under the influence of alcohol, the man will desire the company of his wife, but even that does not work. David becomes desperate and decides to do the ultimate wrong – kill Uriah.

Of course, he did not want to dirty his kingly hands, so he used his commanders to do the deed for him. Unfortunately, they are successful, and the innocent husband is brutally slain for the misdeeds of others. The problem is that the more we fight the truth, the more it tends to turn and bite us, and that bite can hurt a lot. TBC.

Chapter 62

Wrongfully Pursuing Our Desires (Pt. 2)

Previously, we read how David gave in to his carnal desires without regard to the marriage of Bathsheba and her husband, Uriah. In an attempt to hide his sin, he tried to trick Uriah, but when that did not work, he resorted to murder. At this point, he must have felt he got away with it because he married Bathsheba. There is an old saying worth remembering, "What goes around, comes around." As we see with the rest of the story, David had to pay the price for his sin, and the same applies to us. We seldom sin without some kind of retribution by those we sinned against – the law or God Himself.

The Lord sends Nathan to rebuke David, which is devastating for the king. The prophet uses a parable to confront the king. **2Sa. 12:1-7,**

> "...And the Lord sent Nathan to David. He came to him and said, "There were two men in a certain city, the one rich and the other poor. The rich man had very many flocks and herds, but the poor man had nothing but one little ewe lamb, which he had bought. And he brought it up, and it grew up with him and with his children. It used to eat of his morsel and drink from his cup and lie in his arms, and it was like a daughter to him.
>
> Now, there came a traveler to the rich man, and he was unwilling to take one of his own flock or herd to prepare for the guest who had come to him, but he took the poor man's lamb and prepared it for the man who had come to him." Then David's anger was greatly kindled against the man, and he said to Nathan, "As the Lord lives, the man who has done this deserves to die, and he shall restore the lamb fourfold, because he did this thing, and because he had no pity." Nathan said to David, "You are the man!"

We can imagine the guilt and embarrassment overcoming the king as he realized what he had done. Harsh predictions were promised to David because of his adultery. He was told the sword would never depart from his house, his wives would be lost to him, and worst of all, the child born to him by Bathsheba would die. How must he have regretted his sin at that moment! Thankfully, David's particular punishment for his sins no longer applies to us Christians. But that does not mean we will escape the consequences of our actions. One is almost inclined to feel sorry for David, but you must remember what he did to deserve such a harsh punishment.

It is not as if God suddenly stopped loving David, but the sinful actions of his servant, King David, forced God to discipline him. What kind of God would He be if we were allowed to commit such awful sins and get away with it? He had blessed David with delivery from the hands of Saul and made him king over Israel, yet he could not be faithful to the commandments of his Lord. Our sins also come back to bite us. We knowingly sin and expect to get away with it as if God does not see everything. We think that sin committed under the cover of darkness may be overlooked by God, from whom nothing can be hidden. **Heb. 4:13**, "And no creature is hidden from his sight, but all are naked and exposed to the eyes of him to whom we must give account."

And, as in the case of David, sometimes it is a person we know that will confront us with our sin, and then it will be our time to be embarrassed about what we did. We also know from **Heb. 12:6** that "...the Lord disciplines the one He loves and chastises every son whom He receives." so we know that we, too, can occasionally undergo some "corrective" discipline. Even though we would consider David's punishment harsh, the mercy of God was extended to David, and his life was spared due to his sincere repentance.

God is merciful, and through His Son, Jesus Christ, we can always be restored to a right standing before Him. But beware: that does not mean we receive a "Get out of jail free" card. We should learn from the mistakes of those who have gone before us and carefully consider what we are about to do.

Chapter 63

Don't Mock God

"Whoever says 'I know Him' but does not keep His commandments is a liar, and the truth is not in him" (**1Jo 2:4**). Millions of people are Christians in name only. They profess to be so but make no attempt to live an obedient life to God and even less to study His word. Some even call themselves "non-practicing Christians," a wholly delusional statement akin to calling myself a non-practicing neurosurgeon. Of course, they do this simply because they have little or no knowledge of the Bible and think that somehow merely using the term "Christian" reserves a seat in Heaven.

So-called "Christians" make a mockery of God and the Bible when they do not practice Christianity, but they would do well to remember the words of **Gal. 6:7**, "Do not be deceived: God is not mocked." Suppose we see someone falsely claiming to be a military hero. We would not hesitate to accuse them of "stealing honor" and consider them disgraceful – without honor or integrity. The same goes for someone who pretends to be a doctor without the proper training. In fact, the latter probably would be arrested and tried under the law as a fraud, with jail time almost a certainty.

What is the difference between them and non-practicing Christians? Let me tell you. The difference is that those who pretend to be something they are not on earth would, at the most, be disgraced and see jail time, but those who call themselves a Christian and are not face a much, much steeper punishment. **1Jo. 5:2**, "By this we know that we love the children of God when we love God and obey His commandments." Some may even say that obedience is not entirely necessary for salvation, but how do we call ourselves Christians and say we love "children of God" if we do not obey His commandments?

John continues with the following words in **1Jo. 5:3**, "For this is the love of God, that we keep his commandments. And His commandments are not burdensome." Not only does obedience prove our love of His children, but much more importantly, it proves we love God. When someone makes himself a liar by saying, "I know Him," but who does not keep God's commandments, try to reason with them by quoting pertinent scriptures. If that does not work, and a word warning, it often will not because they arrive at the debate with an immovable perspective. Just walk away in love.

They will throw other "relevant" scriptures at the argument and expect you to defend them instead of answering your questions. I see far too many Christians fall into the trap of fierce, emotional arguments with people like that. Certainly, try to reason with them, but concentrate on your salvation first. Make sure that you are not mocking God by pretending to obey His commandments but not doing so. And remember what John said, "His commandments are not burdensome." Mocking God does not result in jail time here on earth, but a forever where you do not want to be.

Chapter 64
The Wisdom to Cut a Child in Half

The book of Ecclesiastes must be one of the most interesting books in the Bible. It is essentially a reflection of a man blessed by God with a higher degree of wisdom than anyone else in his time or after. This is what **1Ki. 4:29-34** has to say about King Solomon,

> "And God gave Solomon wisdom and understanding beyond measure, and breadth of mind like the sand on the seashore, so that Solomon's wisdom surpassed the wisdom of all the people of the east and all the wisdom of Egypt. For he was wiser than all other men, wiser than Ethan the Ezrahite, and Heman, Calcol, and Darda, the sons of Mahol, and his fame was in all the surrounding nations.
>
> He also spoke 3,000 proverbs, and his songs were 1,005. He spoke of trees, from the cedar that grows in Lebanon to the hyssop that grows out of the wall. He also spoke of beasts, birds, reptiles, and fish. And people of all nations came to hear the wisdom of Solomon, and from all the kings of the earth, who had heard of his wisdom."

Did God just randomly bless this man with a more considerable measure of wisdom than anyone else? No! God approached Solomon in a dream and asked what He could give him. This was his reply,

> "Give your servant, therefore, an understanding mind to govern your people, that I may discern between good and evil, for who is able to govern this your great people?" (**1Ki. 3:9**).

Solomon was so concerned with being a just and fair ruler that he unselfishly asked God for wisdom to accomplish this. God was so pleased with Solomon's request for wisdom, not wealth or victories over his enemies, that He gave him more than he asked for.

God had this to say to him in response to his humble request,

"...I give you a wise and discerning mind so that none like you has been before and none like you shall arise after you...I will also do what you have not asked, both riches and honor..." (**1Ki. 3:10-13**).

If you want an example of the use of the gift of superior wisdom, you need to look no further than the verses of **1Ki. 3:16-27** – the story of the two prostitutes who fought over a child. The one prostitute made the following claim in **1Ki. 3:19-20**

"...And this woman's son died in the night because she lay on him. And she arose at midnight and took my son from beside me, while your servant slept, and laid him at her breast, and laid her dead son at my breast."

Solomon told them he would cut the infant into two halves so each mother could have one. One was okay with that, but the other was willing to give up the child to spare his life. Solomon then decreed the infant be returned to the true mother – the one who would instead give up her son than see him come to harm.

Jam. 1:5 tells us that we, too, can ask for wisdom. "If any of you lacks wisdom, let him ask God, who gives generously to all without reproach, and it will be given him." James was referring to the wisdom to overcome trials, but we can also ask for wisdom in other areas of our lives. He also assures us that we will receive it if we ask in faith. Too often, we look to books and self-aggrandizing "gurus" for answers instead of asking God for that gift. If we want it, all we need to do is go down on our knees and ask, and the wisdom we will receive will be much more valuable than the world's.

Chapter 65

Sin Has Consequences

"David said to Nathan, "I have sinned against the Lord." And Nathan said to David, "The Lord also has put away your sin; you shall not die" (**2Sa. 12:13**). This morning, I want to look at the story of David and Bathsheba, and specifically the selected verse. Two things stand out in it. David repents by saying, "I have sinned against the Lord." Nathan lets him know God has forgiven him with the words, "The Lord has put away your sin, you shall not die." What did David do that took only six words to attain forgiveness? Did he steal a loaf of bread or punch someone in the face? Did he use hate speech or gossip behind another's back? Actually, much worse than that.

> **2Sa. 11:2**, "It happened, late one afternoon when David arose from his couch and was walking on the roof of the king's house, that he saw from the roof a woman bathing; and the woman was very beautiful."

It was at this moment that David started to sin. It was then that he allowed his carnal desires to drag him into the depths of sin. After he sends his servants to get her, he ends up "laying" with her, and not long after, she has something to tell him. **2Sa. 11:5**, "...I am pregnant." We can comfortably assume those were not the words he expected to hear because he immediately sets a devious plan into motion.

When we acquiesce to the desires of the flesh, we often face unintended consequences from which we feel the need to escape. It is then that, like David, we need to do whatever it takes to extricate ourselves from the situation we placed ourselves into. In **2Sa. 11:8-13**, we find David inviting Uriah back from the siege of Rabbah. He does this, hoping Uriah will go home and sleep with his wife. If that happened, naturally, the blame for the pregnancy could be placed on him, but as we discover from the verses above, that does not occur. Since Uriah does not do as intended, David is forced, at least in his mind, to do the unthinkable. In **2Sa. 11:15**, we find David instructing the commander of his army to place the unfortunate man in the thick of battle and then leave him there to die.

Sadly, that was accomplished, and David married Bathsheba after her mourning period. Of course, no sin goes unpunished, and God sends Nathan to accuse David and pronounce judgment on him in **2Sa. 12:1-14**. In the first paragraph, I asked, "What did David do that only took six words to be forgiven?" It would be easy to say he committed adultery, and of course, he did, but further investigation proves he broke no less than three of the Ten Commandments." You shall not covet your neighbor's wife," "You shall not commit adultery," and "You shall not murder." According to **Lev. 20:10**, the due punishment for adultery was death – for both parties. But David repents with those six words, and God forgives both parties. Why? Because David was sincere in his repentance.

As punishment, the sword would never depart from his house, evil would rise from within, and he would lose his wives to his neighbor. But that was not the worst that would befall David – the child from the illicit affair would also die - by far the worst of the punishments. Today, the parent's crime is not passed on to the child, thankfully, but that does not mean we will escape just punishment. The moral of the story is this: God will forgive even the most heinous of crimes with genuine, heartfelt repentance, but there will still be a price to pay for our indiscretions – all sin has consequences.

Chapter 66

Christian Friendship

I have great Christian friends who have been there for me through thick and thin. This morning, I want to honor friendship. "Let love be genuine...Love one another with brotherly affection." (**Rom. 12:9**). Are you lucky enough to have friends who love you unconditionally? Friends like that don't care where you are from, your status, or anything else. They love you because they see your value even though you may not. I have brothers and sisters in Christ who have showered me with that kind of love, and if you are one of them, thanks.

"Therefore, confess your sins to one another and pray for one another..." (**Jam. 5:16**). Do you have friends who trust you enough to confide in you and in whom you confide? Do you pray for them, and they for you? I have friends who pray for my family and me daily and trust me as much as I trust them. I share that kind of relationship with my friends, and if you are one of them, thanks. "Bear one another's burdens, and so fulfill the law of Christ." (**Gal. 6:2**). Do you have friends who are willing to bear your burdens with you or even take them away at times? They are there when you are down, reaching out to pick you up and carrying you and your burdens until you have the strength to walk on your own again.

But even then, they do not leave and refuse to let go of the load, just walking next to you in case you stumble again. I have friends like that, and if you are one of them, thanks. "Therefore encourage one another and build one another up, just as you are doing." (**1 Th. 5:11**). Do you have friends who encourage you and build you up? They seem to know just what to say to motivate you to overcome difficulties and drive you on to be the best Christian you can be. I am blessed to have encouragers as friends, and if you are one of them, thanks. "Let the word of God dwell in you richly, teaching and admonishing one another in all wisdom." (**Col. 3:16**).

Do you have friends who sometimes gently and other times sternly admonish you? They have your best interests at heart and aren't afraid to "slap some sense into you" – not because they are mean, but because they want you to be a better person. I have friends like that, and if you are one of them, thanks.

"Love is patient and kind" (**1Co. 13:4**). Do you have friends who bear with your shortcomings with patience and kindness, allowing you to be you despite those shortcomings? They are not easy to find, but I am lucky enough to count my friends among the patient and kind. "...bearing with one another and, if one has a complaint against another, forgiving each other; as the Lord has forgiven you, so you also must forgive." (**Col. 3:13**).

Do you have friends who have had to forgive you for some trespass? They refuse to allow mistakes to trash a good friendship and consider the company more valuable than the mistakes. If you consider my friendship more valuable than my mistakes, thanks. We all have acquaintances we call friends, but you know they are more than that if you have friends like mine. They are brothers and sisters in Christ and **Php. 2:3**, "...count others more significant than yourselves." Thanks for being all this to me, loving me without reservation, and being there during the most challenging times in my life. You have enriched my life.

Chapter 67
Seeking Things That Are Above

"If then you have been raised with Christ, seek the things that are above, where Christ is, seated at the right hand of the Father" (**Col. 3:1**). Far too often, we seek the things of the world. Money, fame, status, and things that are attractive and alluring but have no real value. Instead of that, we need to concentrate on the things above. If we have been raised in Christ, we should begin by putting off our sinful nature: **Col. 2:11**, "...in putting off the body of the sins of the flesh by the circumcision of Christ". We cannot claim to be a child of God if we do not seek that which is from Him.

We know, "Every good gift and every perfect gift is from above, coming down from the Father of lights, with whom there is no variation or shadow due to change." (**Jam. 1:17**), so whatever we seek from above must be pure and perfect. Let's look at scripture to see what we should be seeking. In **Gal. 5:22-23**, we read, "But the fruit of the spirit is love, joy, peace, patience, kindness, goodness, faithfulness, gentleness, (and) self-control...". Those things set us apart from the world; it's not that people of the "world" cannot possess those things, but how they are portrayed is different for a Christian.

Our love, joy, kindness, goodness, etc., are not inward-directed but directed to those around us instead. We revel in how well we treat others, and our happiness stems partly from their happiness. Worldly people, by contrast, seek those things for themselves only. In their quest for self-satisfaction, other people do not matter. Looking upward for the good things that come from God will instill in us the virtues of **Gal. 5:22-23**, as well as humility, loyalty, trustworthiness, and empathy. We do not seek the things of the world like money, fame, status, and recognition, and we don't store our treasures in a bank here on earth.

Our treasures are not money, diamonds, or gold but attitude and character, which are stored elsewhere. **Mat. 6:19-20** tells us the following,

> "Lay not up for yourselves treasures upon earth, where moth and
> rust doth corrupt, and where thieves break through and steal: But

lay up for yourselves treasures in heaven, where neither moth nor rust doth corrupt, and where thieves do not break through nor steal...."

Where you store your treasures is a sure indication of where your heart and eyes are concentrated.

Good traits lead to good things. Seeking those things improves us in ways that cannot be described. It allows us to focus on what matters instead of getting caught up in the petty, fleeting things of the world. Friendships will flourish, and we will positively impact those we encounter. We will make better children to our parents, better parents to our children, better family members, and better friends. We will have integrity, be trustworthy, and be admired for our resoluteness and loyalty. We will be examples of the joy of being a child of God, and people will see Christianity shine before us.

Chapter 68
Why the Door Closes

"For I know the plans I have for you, declares the Lord, plans for welfare and not for evil, to give you a future and a hope." (**Jer. 29:11**). A while back, a lady came to my office and asked to speak to me. She was in some distress, having just lost her job. She felt the future was bleak and could not understand why God would "punish" her. Like her, sometimes things happen to us that make us feel a little confused or even depressed. This is especially true when we do not think we deserve whatever trial has come upon us.

We know God loves us and has our best interests at heart, so why do we question Him when things do not go exactly according to plan? To answer that, we need to understand the concept of "doors." We must know that God will direct our paths to better opportunities as Christians, even if we do not understand it initially. Of course, as humans, we cannot know the future. We can look forward to something significant like a vacation and love "good" surprises. But, oh, when we do not understand it, we have an entirely different emotion.

Let me ask you something, "How many times has something happened to you that looked and felt like a disaster to you, only to discover in hindsight how fortunate that event was?" In the case of the lady in my office, two months later, she found a new job and met her future husband there within a month. When a door closes, it can feel like the end of the world, but when another opens, it can feel like the beginning of "Heaven on Earth." Since we are temporal, we understand the past because we have experienced it. We understand the present with less certainty because we can "mostly" control what happens – until the moment comes when the wheels come off.

For the most part, the future is outside of our grasp. If we could change our present and future perspectives, we would journey through life less stressed. Look at the story of Job. The door did not just close for him – it also seemed locked. But, with faith and obedience, the door that opened provided all he lost and then some. However, I believe that God will close a door for another reason – to prevent you from leaving. Let me explain; sometimes, we start to drift from the path of Christianity. Life happens, and we get too busy for church, or, sadly, we just don't want to bother with it anymore.

The world begins to take hold in our lives as we capitulate to the temptations that lead to sin, which drives a wedge between the Lord and us. The God of love, who sent His only Son to suffer death on the cross to save you, will not forsake you, so He closes the door. What happens when a door closes on us? We become anxious, panicked, and lose hope, but then we often do something—we turn to God. We pray to Him for help, repenting of our sins and promising to do better in the future. If only He will open a door. Then, when we have returned with our heads bowed low in shame and turned from our brief stay in the darkness of sin, we realize we are better off where we are than where we wanted to be.

Chapter 69

Acceptable Worship is Not at Our Discretion

"...and thus let us offer to God acceptable worship, with reverence and awe, for our God is a consuming fire" (**Heb. 12:28**). What is acceptable worship? Is it acceptable to worship outside of the church building? Is it acceptable to dance in the auditorium, speak in tongues, and have women preachers? What about using musical instruments in the worship service and taking communion every quarter? Can we eat and drink in the auditorium, and can we have kids' church? Can we attend in shorts and a tee shirt, or should we wear a suit and tie? Can women have braided hair and fine jewelry, and should they remain silent in church?

Is playing a movie scene as part of the sermon acceptable, and what about the offering – is 10% a requirement or something that is a matter of personal choice? The list of what is acceptable or not is seemingly endless, and most people seem to take the stance of "If I think it is so, it must be so" or "I have seen other churches do it, so it has to be okay." That is a dangerous position since not studying the Bible and coming to a "scripturally sound" conclusion may end badly. Not only for the person introducing practices contrary to the will of God but also for the entire congregation.

No one will be able to say, "I would not have done that if it were not for the church leadership that told us it was okay" on the Day of Judgment. We are not given church leaders to have them study the Bible and then relay its meaning to us. Instead, we are given the Bible to read it, study it, and make sure we do as commanded. **Jos. 1:8** puts it this way,

> "This Book of the Law shall not depart from your mouth, but you shall meditate on it day and night, so that you may be careful to do according to all that is written in it. For then you will make your way prosperous, and then you will have good success."

Even when we attend church services, we are responsible for ensuring that what we hear is correct. **Act. 17:11,**

"Now these Jews were more noble than those in Thessalonica; they received the word with all eagerness, examining the Scriptures daily to see if these things were so."

The responsibility for due diligence is ours, and we should never blindly believe what we hear. The importance of self-study cannot be overemphasized, but far too many people are "scripturally lazy" and drink whatever is handed to them, sometimes risking their salvation in the process. Too many churches are focused on numerical growth at the expense of Christ's doctrines.

Leaders chase numbers for personal financial satisfaction and status, while individuals want to be part of a "big" church. The chase for money and fame or the ignorant decision to do something because someone else does it never has and will never constitute sound reasoning. What needs to happen is careful study and earnest prayer before decisions are made regarding what orderly worship is. We should never make the mistake of thinking that we can decide how God should be worshipped.

The choice is not yours or mine. It is not us but God who decides how we should worship Him, and we have the manual for that in the form of the New Testament. The problem is that many are so intent on personal satisfaction that they will disguise or do away with anything that does not meet their personal desires. We are clearly told how to worship, and we should strive to please God in that regard and not man.

Chapter 70

You Cannot Hate Someone into Church

"But the fruit of the spirit is love, joy, peace, patience, kindness, goodness, faithfulness, gentleness, self-control; against such things there is no law. And those who belong to Christ Jesus have crucified the flesh with its passions and desires" (**Gal. 5:22-24**).

An individual committed to Christianity will live a life that glorifies the Father. They will exemplify the characteristics that set them apart from the world. Their behavior will be consistent with God's desires, and it will act as a magnet to the seeking soul.

People Christians encounter will be intrigued, and some will want to know why they are so composed all the time. Why are they so loving and kind, and why are they so forgiving, even in the face of persecution? It is then that the question, "How can you act so lovingly all the time," or "I wish I had your patience" can be answered with an invitation. Not only does the opportunity exist to invite them to come and hear a gospel sermon, but it also opens the door to a conversation about Jesus.

Conversely, acting like the world with its desire to please the self and trample on competition not only endangers the Christian's salvation but also shuts the door to any evangelistic opportunities with a non-believer. Too often, people put Christ on in baptism but then live like the world. They are "good" Christians on Sundays but act like they are not for the rest of the week. That kind of behavior weakens the opportunity to evangelize because it destroys the allure of Christianity. Those seeking a better way will not be attracted to people who claim to be better and yet act the same as the world. Not only does that make the believers liars, but it makes them worse than the world because they are deceptive.

But worse than that, if you can imagine something worse, is the "Christian" who attacks those who are seeking for their behavior or attitude. They act as if the Church of Christ is a fraternity of the perfect and do not tolerate any weakness or imperfection, even while claiming church is for anyone. Whoa to anyone who dares to dress "immodestly" or lives "sinful" lives. This "president," this "immaculate example," this, dare I say, "Karen of Christianity" will absolutely not tolerate such insidious behavior. When their poor, unfortunate victim is shown that the boundaries of Christianity are so narrow, the "club" so exclusive, and the members so perfect, there will be no desire to "join."

Living a life of obedience to the Scripture and following the command of **Mat. 28:18-20** and **Mar. 16:15** dictate that we have an attitude of acceptance, patience, empathy, and, above all, love. We will never hate anyone into church. Why would anyone desire to come to a place where love appears absent? A place where they are seen as pathetic, inferior souls who can only be saved when they reach a standard that no one could possibly reach. Take them where they are, accept them, love them, and teach them a better way with kindness and gentle words. Make the church a place of God in Christ and not of hate and condemnation.

Chapter 71

Embrace One, Send the Other on Their Way

"Whoever corrects a scoffer gets himself abuse, and he who reproves a wicked man incurs injury. Do not reprove a scoffer or he will hate you" (**Pro. 9:7-8a**). There are two basic types of people who will engage you in conversation. The first kind criticizes everything and has little or no respect for anyone. Their first words to you should immediately place you in a heightened state of awareness because you have dealt with this kind of person previously in your life. If you are discussing an issue, they either outrightly attack your position or disguise the attack with passive-aggressive words.

These individuals will then take your response as unfounded criticism, which will justify the tirade they will launch on you. I have advice for you if you know someone who is angrily defensive at the drop of a hat or uses rage as a go-to in any argument. When someone, especially someone who does not know you, uses insults to belittle you, let it go. Don't let the devil invade your head. Even if you are drawn into the battle, leave it as soon as you realize what is happening. Answer sternly if you must, but then move on. Don't get drawn into long battles with someone who refuses to respect your opinions.

They are not searching for mutually beneficial conversation but rather a verbal fight that quickly spirals into accusations and insults. They will try to trample you because they have no empathy or understanding, and you will never receive an apology. They cannot say "I am sorry" because they see that as a sign of defeat, and they intend to conquer, not grow. These trolls on social media or predators in real life are not worth the time it takes to defend your position. Just allow them to think they have won and move on. Pray for them and continue on with your life.

Then there is the other type of person:

> "...reprove a wise man, and he will love you. Give instruction to a wise man, and he will be still wiser; teach a righteous man, and he will increase in learning" (**Pro. 9:8b-9**).

These individuals will engage you in respectful, albeit heated, conversation from time to time. They understand that differences of opinion result from factors like worldview, location, education, experience, etc., and will consider that when debating you. They may still come across as rough at times but will apologize for their behavior and forgive yours if asked to. They are confident and wise, and much can be learned from them.

Unlike the angry scoffer who is looking for a fight, this person critiques and questions with your best interests at heart. Love motivates them, and empathy is one of their strongest characteristics. Hang on to them because great friendships often result from rough beginnings. Spend your energy on conversations that leave you encouraged and inspired, no matter how brief. Always remember that rational people don't mind if someone disagrees with them and will use the moment as a learning opportunity. Embrace that kind of engagement, but if they are looking for a fight, send them on their way.

Chapter 72

It Is Not Found in the Bible

Here are some things that are not in the Bible but people assume are: The forbidden fruit Adam and Eve ate was an apple. **Gen. 3:6** merely calls it a "fruit":

> "So when the woman saw that the tree was good for food, and that it was a delight to the eyes, and that the tree was to be desired to make one wise, she took of its fruit and ate, and she also gave some to her husband who was with her, and he ate."

The Hebrew word used in that verse is "peri," a generic word for fruit. However, it doesn't indicate which fruit it is, so it is incorrect to assume it was an apple.

The three wise men. **Mat. 2:1-12** only says there were three gifts, not three wise men (magi). Speaking of the magi, please remove them from your nativity scene. They were never at the "manger." Instead, it was the shepherds who visited the birthplace of Jesus. The Magi are believed to have visited Jesus between 12 days and two years after his birth.

A "whale" swallowed Jonah. While some translations (and Veggie Tales) use the word "whale," the Bible only says God sent a "great fish." **Jon. 1:17**, "And the Lord appointed a great fish to swallow up Jonah. And Jonah was in the belly of the fish three days and three nights." We are not told much beyond that, and that leaves some to speculate that God created a fish for the occasion, a giant whale was specially prepared for the task, or a sea dinosaur of some kind was used.

"Money is the root of all evil." Close, but no cigar. **ITi. 6:10** actually states, "The LOVE of money is the root of all KINDS OF evil." And while we are discussing this, let's put another myth to bed.

Mar. 10:25, "It is easier for a camel to go through the eye of a needle than for a rich person to enter the kingdom of God," is not saying that rich people will not go to heaven. It says that rich people find it more challenging because they may allow their riches to become their god.

"This too shall pass." No one knows precisely how this quote started, but it became mainstream in the States when the famed football coach, Mike Dikta, passed it off as a scriptural quote. The closest the Bible comes to that quote is **2Co. 4:17-18,**

> "For this light momentary affliction is preparing for us an eternal weight of glory beyond all comparison, as we look not to the things that are seen but to the things that are unseen. For the things that are seen are transient, but the things that are unseen are eternal."

"Cleanliness is next to Godliness." Again, no one can be sure where that phrase started, but some credit it to John Wesley, who used it in a sermon. It is not found anywhere in the Bible.

"God works in mysterious ways." Another common quote that is not found in God's Word. **Isa. 55:8-9** reminds us that God's ways are not ours, but those words are not used.

"Love the sinner, hate the sin." First quoted by Augustine in the 5th century. These exact words are found nowhere in the pages of the Bible, although the concept is like the words of Gal. **6:1-5.**

"Be in the world, but not of the world" is itself not in the Bible, but is very similar to the words of **Joh. 15:19** "...but because you are not of the world, but I chose you out of the world, therefore the world hates you..."

"God will not give you more than you can handle." This is often quoted to individuals going through challenging or even tragic times. Unfortunately, those exact words do not exist in the Bible. It is a summary of **1Co. 10:13.**

"God helps those who help themselves " is another common saying not found in the Bible. This saying is often used to motivate people to get up and do something, but it is not explicitly taught in the Bible.

Chapter 73

The Ultimate Coward

"For God gave us a spirit not of fear but of power and love and self-control" (**2Ti. 1:7**). Most of us knew of a school bully. We either were the victim, knew someone who was, or shamefully, were a bully ourselves. A bully is the ultimate coward. They use their strength to hide their insecurities by attacking individuals who cannot fight back. I say "individuals" and not "kids" because there are many people who are bullied as adults. It may be a boss or coworker who uses their position of authority to intimidate and torment anyone they don't like. It may be a spouse who bullies their partner, and it may even be a "friend." The latter is passive-aggressive, a bully who intimidates with threats of ending the friendship to control the "friend."

Whatever the circumstance, we all should hate anyone who uses physical, emotional, sexual, or psychological means to torment an innocent individual. Far too many people live in fear because of people like that. The threat of being attacked every day, of having their livelihood, marriage, or friendship threatened by these pernicious bullies, is often the cause of depression. And in the worst cases, torment over long periods can lead to the ultimate perceived forms of escape. Either the victim continues in terror, acquiescing to every demand of their attacker while enduring intolerable anguish, will commit violent acts to try to stop it, or tragically will end their own lives in a desperate attempt to escape the tormentor. None of the aforementioned is a solution, but the psychological damage can lead the individual to fail to see other ways of dealing with it.

Do you know who the biggest bully of all is? The Devil. He will torment his victims, abuse them in any manner possible, and attack them every second of every day to destabilize their relationship with God. And he is always on the hunt, as witnessed by **1Pe. 5:8**, "Be sober-minded; be watchful. Your adversary, the Devil, prowls around like a roaring lion, seeking someone to devour." His weapons are numerous, and his intentions vile, but ultimately, he is as much a coward as those he persuades to do his bullying for him. He knows he has already lost the battle with Christ, so he attacks His followers, whom he thinks are defenseless, but nothing could be further from the truth.

In today's scripture, the spirit spoken of is not the Holy Spirit but a person's attitude or disposition. The Lord does not want us to fear anyone. He does not want us to cower in fear every time a bully appears around the corner. He wants us to have a spirit of power and self-control. We have courage because we have God on our side. Now, I am not advocating "fighting" a bully because violence is never the answer, but we could approach a parent, a trusted person in authority, or a confidant for help.

The approach regarding the Devil is laid out for us in the Bible. Just like in life, resisting the ultimate bully will result in their defeat. **Jam. 4:7** directs Satan's victims. "Submit yourselves therefore to God. Resist the Devil, and he will flee from you." Doing so will set you free from your tormentor.

Chapter 74

The Road Not Taken

"Enter by the narrow gate. For the gate is wide, and the way is easy that leads to destruction, and those who enter by it are many. For the gate is narrow and the way is hard that leads to life, and those who find it are few" (**Mat. 7:13-14**).

I love a poem by Robert Frost, and I want to recite it today, "Two roads diverged in a yellow wood, and sorry, I could not travel both. And be one traveler, long I stood and looked down one as far as I could, to where it bent in the undergrowth; Then took the other, as just as fair, And having perhaps the better claim, Because it was grassy and wanted wear; Though as for that, the passing there Had worn them really about the same, and both that morning equally lay in leaves no step had trodden black.

Oh, I kept the first for another day! Yet knowing how way leads on to way, I doubted if I should ever come back. I shall be telling this with a sigh somewhere ages and ages hence: Two roads diverged in a wood, and I—I took the one less traveled by, And that has made all the difference."

We have a choice to make. We can follow the road that much of the world takes or the one that leads to Heaven. You would think that the choice would be relatively simple, especially when you know the destination of the two roads, and yet it is not. The saddest part for me, by far, is when I see people on the Heavenly highway, eager to please God with their dedication, only to watch them take the "off-ramp" to the worldly one. Then they think that as long as they are on the frontage road that runs parallel to the highway to eternal life, they are fine, but they are not. Every one of those roads will end at some point, and often, it is at a place where you can no longer return to the main road.

There is a song titled "Highway to Hell," and while I do not know the words or even the tune, the title alone should serve as a warning to those standing at the crossroads of their life, deciding which direction to travel.

The one road will be far more attractive and will call you with the power of the alluring song of the mythological "siren" who would lead sailors to their doom. Along that one, you will see bright flashing neon signs, stadiums for the concerts of life that feature you as the only attraction, and beautiful schools that teach life has no future beyond death, so live it any way you please.

The fleeting accolades of the world await you there, and stores that sell anger, hate, pornography, adultery, and a host of other sins for your "pleasure" are everywhere. Power and status drive you as you speed along a smooth road, ever-increasing in speed as you enjoy the fast pace of that life. Sadly, you are racing towards a cliff that you will only discover as you hurtle over the end into an abyss of regret, pain, and anguish. Then there is the other road. This one may not seem all that alluring because you will not be the center of attraction at the expense of everyone else.

Concerts are replaced with churches where God is the feature, and schools teach that there is a life beyond this one that goes on forever. Your accolades await you in Heaven, where you have stored your treasures, and the stores sell love for your fellow man, peace, integrity, faithfulness, and a host of other honorable actions. On this road, you will be driven by humility and honor, but the road will be bumpy and twisty, with steep hills that rise up to challenge your determination.

It will be filled with the potholes of temptation with side roads called desire that lead back to the worldly highway, calling to you with the song of the Siren. The end of that road will be a place of pain-free happiness, bliss, and peace in a place whose beauty cannot be rivaled or even imagined. (**1Co. 2:9**). If you are at the crossroads, choose the one less traveled; if you are on the worldly road, find an exit, even if it is unpaved and bumpy. Escape while you can.

Chapter 75

Satan's Swarms of Temptation and Sin

"A beautiful heifer is Egypt, but a biting fly from the north has come upon her. Even her hired soldiers in her midst are like fattened calves; yes, they have turned and fled together; they did not stand, for the day of their calamity has come upon them, the time of their punishment" (**Jer. 46:20-21**).

In these verses, the danger of the Chaldeans coming to overthrow the Egyptian nation is referred to, but the analogy applies to us today. No, we are not under imminent threat by another country, but as Christians, we need to remain vigilant because our enemy is constantly seeking to destroy us.

It is not as if Satan will rise up with one colossal army and come and destroy us because that is obvious and easier to resist. Rather than doing that, he will deploy swarms of less obvious attacks like the biting flies to wear us down until we submit to sin. In other words, we must be careful of the small things that come in swarms. Like swarms of locusts that devour everything before them, the swarms of temptations and sin will lead us to destruction. "Small" but regular fits of anger, "tidbits" of gossip all the time, and "kinda" defaming of a person or group from time to time will begin to deconstruct our spiritual defenses.

The same can be said for "irregularly" giving in to the allure of pornography, allowing ourselves to be drawn into flirtatious moments with someone "from time to time," and letting other sins overpower us "now and then." Any of those things can be problematic for a Christian, but imagine combining more than one at a time. Deconstructing our spiritual defenses by allowing ourselves to act in the ways above will lead to the enemy defeating us. That is what the writer of **Jer. 14:20** warns. Swarms of small temptations, not always, but enough times to have sin chip away at our resolve like biting flies attacking a beautiful heifer.

When we commit obvious sins like beating someone, stealing a vehicle, or slandering someone vocally in public, it is blatant, but it is not those sins that are Satan's most effective weapons. No, it is the small ones that we are almost unaware of that will, like a virus, attack us silently with an army. It will deploy this army to our lungs, throat, head, muscles, and other organs until we are weakened and unable to resist the onslaught. It is then that the virus brought on by the biting of the insect will take over and destroy us, resulting in severe disease that, left untreated, could result in death.

Rom. 6:23 has this to say about sin, "For the wages of sin is death..." and we would do well to remember that even as we remain vigilant of the enemies' swarms of biting flies. We can never let our guard down because the attack is constant and relentless. Thankfully, for Christians, there is a solution. We do not have to live in fear of those attacks because we have the cure – Christ. We have the ability not just to swat the flies but to "Put to death therefore what is earthly in (us)." (**Col. 3:5**).

No spiritual disease that is passed on to us by the biting of the swarms of temptations will be able to defeat us, but even when we have been overrun, we have the medicine to cure us of our illness. In fact, we have the armor that, like a beekeeper's suit, will protect us from any bites in the first place.

Chapter 76
Sons and Daughters of the Most High

"You have heard that it was said, 'You shall love you neighbor and hate your enemy.' But I say to you, love you enemy and pray for those who persecute you, so that you may be sons to your Father who is in heaven" (**Mat. 5:43-45**).

Honestly, which one of us wants to do that? Last year in Texas, a young man was killed in his apartment by a policewoman. That young man's brother was so pure of heart, so committed to His savior that he did the unthinkable for many people – he forgave her. That is not all that common.

Their hatred for that person will be overwhelming, and they would revel in a guilty verdict, furious if the perpetrator does not receive the punishment they think fits the crime. Hate is easy; love is quite the opposite. We are surrounded by those who would commiserate with us when we direct our fury at the object of our hatred. We often sympathize with those who hate their enemies. Jesus does not want us to indulge in that type of behavior. If we are indeed sons of our Father in Heaven, we will treat our enemies the way He would want us to. Often, we need to go through a process before we eventually reach the point where we can pray for them, let alone forgive them.

Also, let me ask you a question now. "Are you even expected to forgive someone who has not expressed any remorse for the crime they have committed? In **Mat. 5:46-47**, Jesus asks the following,

"For if you love those who love you, what reward do you have? Do not even the tax collectors do the same? And if you greet only your brothers, what more are you doing than others? Do not even the Gentiles do the same?"

As Christians, we are called to a different standard. We are expected to act contrary to the flesh – which can be incredibly hard. Who wants to pray for the person who is bullying you at school?

Who wants to pray for the person who is abusing you daily or the two-faced person who gossips about you? But we should, and for good reasons. You know the old saying, "Doing good is its reward." Well, loving and praying for our enemies also comes with a huge reward. Listen to the words of Jesus in **Luk. 6:32-33, 35,**

> "If you love those who love you, what benefit is that to you? For even sinners love those who love them. And if you do good to those who do good to you, what benefit is that to you? For even sinners do the same...But love your enemies, and do good, and lend, expecting nothing in return, and your reward will be great, and you will be sons of the Most High..."

While we might not receive direct rewards here on earth, we can be assured that our good deeds do not go unnoticed by our Father in Heaven. We are not the first to pray for those who hate us. "And Jesus said, "Father, forgive them, for they know not what they do." And they cast lots to divide his garments." If Jesus could do that after suffering beatings, mockery, and abuse, we, too, should have the courage to do the same.

Chapter 77

Will You Accept the Sacrifice?

"...but God shows his love for us in that while we were still sinners, Christ died for us" (**Rom. 5:8**). After reading this, anyone will probably say, "Amen." It surely is one of the most beautiful scriptures in the Bible for any person in the world. And I say "any person" because it does not say Christ died for the remorseful or the believer, but for those who are "still" sinners. The ramification of the verse is evident; the possibility of our salvation was assured by an act of Jesus long before we deserved it, and the promises attached to it are eternal. That means that the hope of an eternity with God is open to anyone who is willing to accept it.

Paul will continue that thought with the words of **Rom. 5:9-10**,

> "Since, therefore, we have now been justified by his blood, much more shall we be saved by him from the wrath of God. For if while we were enemies we were reconciled to God by the death of his Son, much more, now that we are reconciled, shall we be saved by his life."

The agony of the cross, marked by Christ's blood, justified us and opened the door to our salvation. Christ died for us primarily to become the sin sacrifice for all of humanity, appeasing God's rightful anger against fallen men—you and me included. Another way of saying that is that Christ was the propitiation for our sins.

And the best part is that there is no price attached to it. We are not asked to study the Bible for a test we must pass before we can avail ourselves of salvation. We do not have to give a certain amount of money to the church or do a certain amount of good works in the community before we can grab onto the promises attached to Christ's death. In fact, **Eph. 2:8** says, "For, by grace, you have been saved through faith. And this is not your own doing; it is the gift of God...." It is not of our own doing, but something is given to us freely by the mercy and grace of God.

We do not have to be clever, rich, good-looking, educated, or courageous – we just need to believe and then act on that belief. His life for ours – wow!

The life of the perfect for the life of the imperfect. That, brothers and sisters, is the epitome of true love. But why would God sacrifice His only Son to offer us the opportunity to be saved? **Joh. 3:16** probably says it best, "For God so loved the world, that he gave his only Son, that whoever believes in him should not perish but have eternal life." God loves His creation so much that despite our apparent weakness and tendency to rely on ourselves,

He was willing to sacrifice His Son for us. Think about the magnitude of that love for a second. Also, each member of the Trinity had a part to play in this ultimate spiritual drama. God loved us so much that He offered His Son to save us, and then He gave us the Holy Spirit to accompany us on our journey through our brief life on earth. The only question is, "Will you accept the sacrifice?" Will you grab onto God's love and avail yourself of Christ's sacrifice?

Chapter 78

Patiently Wait for God to Hand You Your Jericho

"By faith the walls of Jericho fell down after they had been encircled for seven days" (**Heb. 11:30**). There can be no doubt that Jericho's fall was an act of faith. There are other interesting things to learn from that story in **Jos. 6:1-21**, as well. When you read it, you cannot miss two things – God's timing and His perseverance in the face of overwhelming odds. God does things according to His timetable, not ours. God is patient. We live in a world that is all about speed. McDonald's and other fast-food companies can have your food ready by the time you have paid for your order.

Sometimes, Amazon can deliver products to you within a few days, and even on the same day, in certain instances. We live in a world that demands things get done ever quicker. Even patients who have had serious surgeries can go home much sooner than one would think possible. Everything is about speed, speed, speed. That can be great when you are waiting for the new "whatever" you recently purchased online or are particularly hungry, but that same "need for speed" often gets you into trouble. The "get-it-done-yesterday" attitude has resulted in impatience. Many people are no longer willing to wait till the time is right for something to happen, and they demand that whatever they need or want is done without hesitation.

Let's say someone applies for a new job somewhere. They half-heartedly research the company and then put all their eggs in that basket. They write their resumes to impress the recruiter, even if they have to "fluff" the details a little to suit the position. But, because they did not wait for the best opportunity, it did not take long for them to become disillusioned, and they became just as unhappy as they were in their last job. God sees the future; we do not. The advantage is that He does not just open the first door we walk up to. Sometimes, it is not even the second, third, or fourth one. We may have to wait for the tenth one, but we will love the outcome if we trust God's timing.

The second thing we discover when reading the passage is that "perseverance pays"—something closely linked to God's timing. We must continue the fight until the war is won, even if a battle or two is lost along the way. Joshua and his army had to persevere for seven days. Now, that may not seem like a long time to you, but imagine just marching around the city once a day for six days and then seven times on the seventh day. That must have felt like a lot of doing nothing, and who would blame any of them for asking "Why?" during that time? But, because they listened, they received the prize they aimed for – the fall of Jericho.

We all have our own Jericho. We face what appears to be impossible odds, just like the fortified city facing the Israelites. We call out to God to give us victory in the form of that new job, the man or woman of our dreams to marry, or victory over disease, praying He will hear us. Of course, God hears the pleas of His children, but do we take the time to listen to what He is directing us to do? Are we prepared to trust Him? Are we prepared to walk around our "Jericho" for seven days, following His directions until we are handed the victory?

Chapter 79

When You Are Considered Defective

"For you save a humble people, but the haughty eyes you bring down" (**Psa. 18:27**). If I took a hundred-dollar bill and asked you if you would like it, how many of you would say "Yes." I think it would be safe to assume that most people would be more than willing to relieve me of it. But what if I took that hundred-dollar bill and folded it before offering it to you; would you still want it? If I took, folded, and crumbled it, would you still be willing to take it from me? Would you take it if I threw it on the ground and stomped on it several times? I can see the outstretched hands in my mind, not caring in the least that I inflicted some damage to it.

Because you all know that the actual value did not change despite my best efforts, you would not hesitate for a second to pocket the money. In the same way that $100 held its value, so do you. The world will fold you. It will crumble or stomp on you, and then it will want nothing more to do with you because of your "decreased value." That is because the world is fickle and will not take responsibility for what it does. Let's say you are in an abusive relationship. For years, you endure torment as the perpetrator damages you physically and psychologically. Maybe you are in school or college and are being bullied without remorse.

Or perhaps other adverse life events have affected you in ways most people will never understand, and you develop anxiety or depression. When that happens, the world will discard you like a worthless piece of trash, even though it may be the cause of the pain and damage in the first place. You were lifted up and considered beautiful at birth, but now you are labeled ugly, defective, and worthless. Opportunities will vanish like the mist on a clear sunny morning, and "friends" will disappear even quicker. The once-loyal friends will now throw sideways glances at you as you pass, gossiping about your "lack of control" and making other horrible statements about being weak and pathetic.

Your place of honor at the table of society will be taken from you, and you will be relegated to the farthest, dark, lonely corner of the room. It does not matter that life folds, crumbles, or stomps on you; your value never diminishes in the eyes of God. In fact, your experiences increase your value to Him. Your lowly, humble place on the totem pole of the world will be an elevated place of honor in the eyes of God. Your physical, mental, or emotional state does not determine his love for you. Do you remember the story of the Rich man and Lazarus in Luk. 16? The poor man who had nothing was so overlooked that he "... desired to be fed with what fell from the rich man's table..." (**Luk. 16:21**), but he ended up in paradise.

Your value to God is immeasurable. Your intrinsic worth is more than all the gold and diamonds on earth. Don't let the devil devalue you by renting space in your head. He did not form you or give His Son so that you may have the hope of an eternity in Heaven. It was not he, but God, who created you in His image. "You formed my most inward parts: You knitted me together in my mother's womb" (**Psa. 139:13**). It is the world that has discarded the beauty of His creation and put on the ugly, haughty, proud, egocentric, and violent nature of Satan. The world considers you defective, but you are not – it is.

Chapter 80

Real Beauty

"Charm is deceitful, and beauty is vain, but a woman who fears the Lord is to be praised" (**Pro. 31:30**). This morning's article follows yesterday's "When You Are Considered Defective." Beauty is defined by society, and the media drives the stereotype. And let's not forget the advent of social media filters that now allow almost any average person to be "filtered" to look absolutely stunning and nearly flawless. We are often told that those models, movie actresses, singers, and influencers are the epitome of beauty. They are the gold standard, and everyone else is "less than that."

Thousands of magazines, with the covers adorned by these men and women, instill in our minds what the definitive understanding of beauty should be. Social media sites and the trickery of those filters further influence the idea of what human "perfection" is. Millions of young girls, boys, women, and men stand in awe of these people, snapping pictures, begging for autographs, and screaming their names in frantic adoration when they see them. Scores of young children and teens flock to stores and pharmacies to buy products endorsed by their idols in an effort to mimic their style.

Unfortunately, some fans will hurt themselves physically and psychologically in that quest. The urge to be like them, adored as they are adored, and live rich, happy lives like their idols appear to be the cause of much pain. Some will develop eating disorders like bulimia or anorexia because they become disillusioned by what they perceive as shortcomings in their body type. People do not know that the lives of the "gods" of beauty and style are often not that happy at all.

Beneath the fake, happy exterior is a life that struggles to come to terms with the riches and what society expects of them, often leading to depression as they search for meaning and privacy. And what have these "beauties" really done to deserve the accolades of the legions of adoring fans? Usually, nothing more than singing a song, sauntering across a runway, or pretending to be someone else in a movie, commonly dressed in less than modest outfits to garner attention. Many of these men and women are superficial, egocentric maniacs driven by worldly riches and hedonistic lifestyles that frequently include illicit drugs and alcohol.

But there is another kind of beauty that far exceeds that of these narcissistic egomaniacs. It is beauty derived from within, and its source is humility. It is a beauty that often speaks of pain, suffering, and overcoming hardships that you and I cannot even begin to imagine. It is a beauty that speaks volumes about perseverance and one that is centered on giving more than receiving. Sometimes, the giving is without their knowledge, as their very presence encourages everyone they meet. Their pain is hidden from us, even though we know it is there.

They are rare, beautiful gifts from the Father in Heaven, given to us to share on this earth for some time. They brighten every second, celebrate life and love, and radiate a strength that invigorates us and puts a smile on our faces. Their essence exudes a beauty that words cannot begin to describe. That is real beauty.

Chapter 81

Quadrupeds "Must" Be Proof of Evolution

"Then God said, 'Let us make man in our image, after our likeness. And let them have dominion over the fish of the sea and over the birds of the heavens and over the livestock and over all the earth and over every creeping thing that creeps on the earth.' So God created man in his own image, in the image of God he created him; male and female he created them" (**Gen. 1:26-27**).

Several years ago, an absolutely sensational discovery was made and revealed on 60 Minutes in Australia. It was described as "...an absolute sensation: One that could have untold significance for every one of us".

The presenter further drew the audience in with these words, "You're about to meet a family that shouldn't exist. A family like no other. They could just be the missing link between man and ape. The holy grail scientists have sought for generations". I "rolled my eyes" but had to watch the rest to see how they came to that conclusion. What followed was nothing short of evolutionary fantasy. A Turkish family comprising two parents and 18 children was introduced to the audience. Four of the children suffered from slight to severe mental retardation, and they were also quadrupeds– they walked on all fours.

The presenter used phrases like "living fossils" and "human beings who had never made the evolutionary leap of standing upright" to explain the strange behavior of the four adults. According to her, scientists needed to converge on the family and investigate these quadrupeds to "discover what it means to be human." Once they brought an evolutionary psychologist into the team, things really got interesting. From that moment on, a cocktail of suppositions led to fanciful hypotheses or, in my opinion, complete drivel.

The exaggerated speculation without any credible evidence was forced upon the audience as an evolutionary explanation of the existence of these unfortunate souls. The "scientists" claimed these four adults were the missing link and a rare glimpse into human evolutionary history. True to sensationalistic, emotionally driven reporting, questions like "So why, for the first time in eons, are human beings again walking on four?" were served up to the viewer to stimulate their interest further. And to be honest, that question was intriguing. Then, the apparent scientific answer was quickly glossed over in favor of the "missing link" theory again.

The parents were second cousins who probably passed recessive genes to six of their children – 4 of whom were quadrupeds. To be honest, the answer wasn't a massive surprise to anyone with half a belief in God, but the force with which the "missing link" theory was proposed, almost as fact, was preposterous. Not only that, but it felt like these poor souls were being exploited for sensationalistic reasons because of their unfortunate handicaps.

Of course, that fact absolutely escaped the unmovable, preconceived minds of those who hang on to the imaginary "monkey-to-man" fairy tales. The only subscribers to this ridiculous theory are the delusional who believe that it is more probable that nothing made the universe than an omnipotent, eternal God. But, for Christians, it was just a sad exploitation of the most vulnerable who did not have the choice of being used as a pawn in some larger debate about the origins of humanity. Shameful and disgraceful, in my opinion. **Psa. 14:1** "A fool says in his heart, 'There is no God.'"

Chapter 82

Famous Last Words

"Jesus said to him, 'Truly, I tell you, this very night, before the rooster crows, you will deny me three times.' Peter said to him, 'Even if I must die with you, I will not deny you!' And all the disciples said the same" (**Mat. 26:34-35**)."

If there was ever an example of the expression, "Famous last words," this is it. Jesus and the disciples were at the Mount of Olives, and He had just told them they would all "fall away" because of Him that very night. I can almost see the indignant, impulsive disciple Peter sneer at what he considered a preposterous statement by Jesus. Of course, as told in Luk, we all know how that turned out. **22:54-62**, but at the time, he was convinced of his loyalty – even to the point of death.

Peter did exactly as Jesus foretold and vehemently denied His Savior three times before being so ashamed that he "wept bitterly."

Peter had spent years with Jesus and had seen Him perform miracles on multiple occasions. And who can forget the story in **Mat. 14:22-33**. The disciples were in a boat when a storm arose and "buffeted" it. Shortly before dawn, Jesus approached the terrified disciples, who cried out, "It's a ghost." Jesus assured them He was their Lord and invited Peter to come to Him after the former uttered these words, "...Lord, if it is you, command me to come to you on the water" (**Mat.14:28**). Of course, we know that Peter had hardly stepped out of the boat when he saw the wind, became afraid, and started sinking. Jesus grabbed his hand to save him, saying, "...You of little faith,"... "Why did you doubt?"

After everything he had seen and done when the moment of truth came, Peter did not step up to the plate – he merely cowered in fear and denied his Savior. The fact is that most of us follow the example of Peter – if not in words, then at least in actions. Sometimes, we do so knowingly, and other times without even being aware of it. We act a certain way in church and then entirely differently when away from it. We don't want people to know, or we simply "forget" we are Christians. We act and speak like the world, using foul language, telling crude jokes, and, in doing so, "deny" our Christianity.

Then, on Sunday, we return to our senses and act all righteous again – only to repeat the process that week. And what's worse is that we do that hundreds, if not thousands of times. If we repeat that often enough, it will become second nature, and we will not even know we are guilty anymore. Is that not a form of denying Him? We may not necessarily curse and tell crude jokes and may even judge those we see doing so, but then we disparage and hate people, making us guilty of it anyway.

There is more than one way to deny Christ, but we should make it one of our primary goals never to do so. If Christ was willing to go to the cross for us, why would we do anything but be loyal to Him? Did His agony not free us from the Old Law and ultimately defeat death? Did His sacrifice not open the door to the promise of the hope of eternal life? And yet we choose to deny Him by our actions, all the while judging Peter for His shameful act of denying Jesus. Shame on us – if we act that way, we should do as Peter did and "weep bitterly."

Chapter 83

Don't Give Your Anger to the Devil

"Be angry and do not sin; do not let the sun go down on your anger, and give no opportunity to the devil" (**Eph. 4:26-27**). The beginning of today's verse seems to contradict **Col. 3:8**, "But now you must put them all away: anger, wrath, malice, slander, and obscene talk from your mouth." And it is not only that verse, but many others in the Old and New Testaments indicate that we should not be angry, so what does Paul mean, and is he contradicting God's word? The answer is found in the following four words, so let's look at the grammatical meaning of all six words. "Be angry" is an imperative, "and" is a conjunction, and "do not sin" is a prohibition.

That may sound like a lot, so let's unpack it for the sake of clarity. An imperative serves as a warning or an instruction, a conjunction is a connector, and a prohibition is an order to stop. Considering all that, the meaning is, "You can be angry, but only when that anger is righteous and does not cause you to sin." Anger that has a purpose and is controlled is not a sin, but when it is emotionally uncontrolled, vengeful, or wrathful, it is. We must be careful not to let our anger lead us into sin. When a child does something wrong, and we punish them suitably, it is for their own good.

But punishing them in the heat of the moment and allowing extreme anger to control our actions can lead to harsher than necessary measures and even abuse. Paul then goes on to clarify his thought by saying we should not allow the sun to go down on our anger. In other words, we should address the issue and "move on." When anger is allowed to fester, it can cause extreme responses. Anger that is not allowed to dissipate leads to opportunity for the Devil. Think of a situation concerning a family member or friend. At first, this person is righteously angry, but as the feeling is held onto, it grows from a seed into something much bigger.

Before long, things are said or done that should not have been, and suddenly, a once-loving relationship dissolves, and the parties no longer speak to each other. They may never talk to each other again. The love they once shared is forced out as hatred is allowed to take over like a weed that suffocates a beautiful rose garden. We all know that there is a time and place for righteous anger. Our Lord and Savior became angry with sellers in the temple, but He never stopped loving and forgiving those who repented. When the person is sorry for their actions, we should release them from their prison of anger in our minds.

Not only will they be freed, but we, too, will be freed. Anger given to the Devil as an opportunity will weigh us down like an anchor in an ocean of rage and hatred until we drown in it. So, when Paul says, "...put them all away: anger, wrath, malice, slander, and obscene talk from your mouth," he speaks of that kind of anger. "Whoever is slow to anger has great understanding, but he who has a hasty temper exalts folly." (**Pro. 14:29**). Instead of letting your temper control you, you control the situation. Don't give your anger to the Devil to do with as he wishes; nothing good will come of it.

Chapter 84

Why Waste Your Time?

"All Scripture is breathed out by God and profitable for teaching, for reproof, for correction, and for training in righteousness..." (**2Ti. 3:16**). A few years ago, a wildly popular digital game took the world by storm. It was called "Pokemon Go" – and boasted 21 million downloads within a few months of its release. At the pinnacle of its popularity in 2015, a mind-blowing 250 million people played it monthly. The game's goal was to download the Pokemon Go app and then use your smartphone to look for Pokemon characters that did not exist. That's right; you had to look for characters that did not exist by traveling around your city, state, or country to capture them.

You could then trade the characters that did not exist for candy/prizes that did not exist. You could even enter a gym that did not exist to fight other gamers' characters that, you guessed it, did not exist. People have even died crossing streets while intently looking at their smartphones to spot a character. There are also reports of a few couples getting divorced because one of them became so obsessed with the game. Some villains even hid in remote areas and attacked unsuspecting players because they knew they would come looking for those characters. No other game in history has been "bigger" than Pokemon Go. The average time players spent online playing the game was 12 hours a day.

Can you imagine if there was an app called "Bible Go" with 250 million users playing it daily for an average of 12 hours? Now, that would be something. I can never understand why someone would invest so much time in a game with no lasting value. Why not spend that energy on the one thing with the biggest prize of all? After all, the reward of spending that kind of time dedicated to Christ will allow you to collect rewards for eternity instead of some make-believe prize. Instead of fictional characters, you will receive invaluable information to help you navigate the minefields called temptation and sin - information that will serve you in tangible ways in the real world.

Many of the same people who spent hours a day playing the game would not spend five minutes reading their Bibles or praying. They still know the names of those pointless little gaming characters that do not exist but know almost nothing of the actual characters in the Bible. They became excited and messaged, texted, and talked to anyone who cared to listen to them as they carried on about that "amazing" game, and some even had Pokemon Go parties. They invited friends to drive around with them to catch these nonexistent characters but could not speak to their friends about Christ, much less invite them to church.

Unfortunately, the addiction trapped not only teens but also many adults. Something is wrong with the world when people are more interested in catching and trading fictional characters than knowing the Bible. Why would you waste so much time doing nothing constructive rather than learning about and working toward your salvation? I am pretty sure gamers will not be able to trade Pokemon Go characters for salvation points in Heaven.

Chapter 85
God Will Get Your Attention

"And the Lord appointed a great fish to swallow up Jonah. And Jonah was in the belly of the fish three days and three nights" (**Jon. 1:17**). When God wants to speak to you, He will get your attention. God had spoken to Jonah and instructed him to go and "call out" the people of Nineveh for their evil ways, but Jonah had other plans. He didn't want to go, so he devised a pretty good plan, at least in his mind: he would run. **Jon. 1:3,**

> "But Jonah rose to flee to Tarshish from the presence of the Lord. He went down to Joppa and found a ship going to Tarshish. So he paid the fare and went down into it, to go with them to Tarshish, away from the presence of the Lord."

Yep, he would jump aboard the ship and hide.

Maybe when the "heat" had died down, he would return to his city and continue living there in peace. What was He thinking? Was the God of all creation too busy to look for Him, or was He incapable of seeing as far as Tarshish? Talk about a lesson in futility. No sooner were they out to sea than a great wind was "hurled" by the Lord, causing a tempest to arise and scaring the wits out of the mariners. After praying hopelessly to their false Gods, they woke Jonah and asked him why he was not praying to His God. After explaining that he worshiped the one true God, lots were drawn, and it was decided he would be thrown overboard – something he had suggested to them. And that is where our story really starts today. When we think we can outrun the Lord or find a place far enough away from His sight that we cannot be found, He will put us in a place where we must pay attention.

Can you imagine being thrown overboard by your friends, only to be swallowed by a fish large enough to gulp you down in one go? I imagine it was initially terrifying for Jonah since he must have thought he would die in the fish. However, God had other plans for him. You would think that that lowly place is as far down as you can go. That deep, dark place that seems just one tiny step away from death with no hope of escape is where you have only one option.

When the Devil's shouts drown out the whispers of the Lord, He will put us in a quiet place. He will then take our place of despair and turn it into a place of hope. That place where we only hear the whisper of God will be where Christ will grab our hand and pull us out of the belly of our fish.

Our prayers will be most sincere there, and we will know that Christ is our only salvation. When Elijah fled the wrath of Jezebel, he ended up in a cave and was instructed to stand on the mount before the Lord. After a great and strong wind, an earthquake, and a fire did not produce the Lord, a sound of a low whisper was heard. In that low whisper, Elijah heard the Lord speak to Him. Jonah could not hear the voice of the Lord because the Devil was shouting in Jonah's ear to hide from God. God then put Jonah in that place where he would hear the whisper. The same applies to us. We don't hear God audibly; God will put us where we are alone, there are no distractions, and we only have one way to look.

Then, we will hear the whisper of God, pray earnestly, and see His outstretched hands, ready to save us. It may be perseverance to continue in faith, the courage to face our fears, the strength to escape, or it may be friends and loved ones who become the outstretched hand of Christ and pull us out of that place of despair.

Chapter 86
Wishing Others Ill is Not Wise

"Now the word of the Lord came to Jonah the son of Amittai, saying, "Arise, go to Nineveh, that great city, and call out against it, for their evil has come up before me." But Jonah rose to flee to Tarshish from the presence of the Lord. He went down to Joppa and found a ship going to Tarshish. So he paid the fare and went down into it, to go with them to Tarshish, away from the presence of the Lord" (**Jon. 1:1-3**).

It is amusing that Jonah thought he could run from the Lord. For some unknown reason, the prophet of God believed the city of Tarshish was farther than God could see.

Today, I want to look at why he tried to escape the presence of the Almighty in the first place. The answer is not given immediately in the book, and we will have to read all the way to the last chapter to find it. **Jon. 4:2**,

"And he prayed to the Lord and said, "O Lord, is not this what I said when I was yet in my country? That is why I made haste to flee to Tarshish, for I knew that you are a gracious God and merciful, slow to anger and abounding in steadfast love and relenting from disaster."

We know Assyria was the enemy of Judea and Israel, and Jonah evidently had no love for the Assyrians. He also knew that God would forgive them, and he was not up for that.

He decided they were not worthy of mercy and was so angry at God for eventually granting repentance to them that he even wished himself dead. So, just to be clear, Jonah was not fearful and upset that he would be ineffective, but rather that he would succeed. How crazy is that? The sad thing is that we often act that way as well. If someone does something to us that hurts us or because of their race, nationality, sex, or worldview, we consider them enemies and only desire the worst for them. We thank Him almost daily for the blessing of mercy, yet we do not want others to receive that same mercy.

How much can you possibly hate someone that you can wish an eternity of despair and anguish on them? We are told this in **Mat. 7:1**, "Judge not, that you be not judged." Who are we to judge someone? Who are we that we can withhold God's gift of eternal life in heaven from someone?

We would do well to read **Mat. 7:2-5,**

> "For with the judgment you pronounce you will be judged, and with the measure you use it will be measured to you. Why do you see the speck that is in your brother's eye, but do not notice the log that is in your own eye? Or how can you say to your brother, 'Let me take the speck out of your eye,' when there is the log in your own eye? You hypocrite, first take the log out of your own eye, and then you will see clearly to take the speck out of your brother's eye."

We injure ourselves spiritually in our haste to declare someone unworthy, point out their mistakes, and judge them unworthy of God's grace. Christ did not only die for you and me. His sacrifice on the cross was not for the select few, of which you and I are recipients, but for every human being on earth. In **Mat. 28:19**, We are not told in the great commission to "go out and make disciples of all whom you deem worthy," but to "Go therefore and make disciples of all nations, baptizing them in the name of the Father and of the Son and of the Holy Spirit...." Save who you can.

Chapter 87

If You Believe the Bible, this is Profound

"All Scripture is breathed out by God and profitable for teaching, for reproof, for correction, and for training in righteousness, that the man of God may be complete, equipped for every good work." (**2Ti. 3:16**).

It may seem a bit redundant after the first one or two verses, but bear with me and read them all because they are amazing. One of my favorite things to do is read **Isa. 42-48**. It is remarkable how often God refers to Himself in those chapters, but two other places are worthy of special mention as well, so I will start with them as a warm-up to Isaiah.

Exo. 3:14; "God said to Moses, 'I am who I am.'" And he said, 'Say this to the people of Israel: I am has sent me to you.'"; **Lev. 19:12**, "You shall not swear by My name falsely, and so profane the name of your God: I am the Lord.";
Isa. 42:6, "I am the Lord..."; **42:8**, "I am the Lord"; **43:3**, "For I am the Lord your God, the Holy One..." **43:11**, "I, I am the Lord, and besides Me there is no savior."; **43:12**, "...and I am God."; **43:13**, "Also henceforth I am He; there is none who can deliver from My hand; I work, and who can turn it back?"; **43:15**, "I am the Lord, your Holy One...";

Isa. 43:25, "I, I am He who blots out your transgressions for My own sake...." **44:6**, "I am the first and I am the last; besides Me there is no god."; **44:24**, "Thus says the Lord, your Redeemer, who formed you from the womb: "I am the Lord, who made all things, who alone stretched out the heavens, who spread out the earth by myself..."; **45:3**, "...it is I, the Lord..."; **45:5**, "I am the Lord, and there is no other, besides Me there is no God."; **45:6**, "...there is none besides Me; I am the Lord, and there is no other."; **45:7**, "I am the Lord, who does all these things.";

Isa. 45:8, "...I the Lord have created it."; **45:18**, "For thus says the Lord, who created the heavens (He is God!), who formed the earth and made it (He established it; He did not create it empty, He formed it to be inhabited!): 'I am the Lord, and there is no other.'"; **45:19**, "I the Lord speak the truth; I declare what is right." **45:21**, "Who declared it of old? Was it not I, the Lord? And there is no other god besides Me, a righteous God and a Savior; there is none besides Me;" **45:22**, "...For I am God, and there is no other.";

Isa. 46:4, "...I am He."; **46:9**, "...for I am God, and there is no other; I am God, and there is none like Me."; **48:12**, "I am He; I am the first, and I am the last."; **48:17**, "I am the Lord your God, who teaches you to profit, who leads you in the way you should go." In case you are interested, it is 23 times. Now, you may be asking why I took the time to do this today.

Was I lazy and just decided to jot down some verses to fill the space? No, actually, it took longer to copy and paste them than if I had just written an article from scratch. The answer is in the initial verse, 2Ti. 3:16. If we believe that verse, we believe in the Bible's authenticity, authority, and inerrancy. And if we believe that, we will be struck with the repetition of something so obvious, but God had a purpose. He was setting permanently in the minds of His people who He was.

He wanted it to be indelibly printed on their hearts and stored in the furthest reaches of their minds that He is God. However, the real beauty is that He tells you and me the same thing. He is our only God, and there is no other besides Him.

Chapter 88

Be What You Want Them to Be

"And these words that I command you today shall be on your heart. You shall teach them diligently to your children and shall talk of them when you sit in your house, and when you walk by the way, and when you lie down, and when you rise. You shall bind them as a sign on your hand, and they shall be as frontlets between your eyes. You shall write them on the doorposts of your house and your gates" (**Deu. 6:6-9**).

What makes a good father? Many men have sired children, but that does not automatically make them good fathers. Many men are competent in that role, but no one should ever rest on his laurels; instead, they should strive to do better every day.

There are certain characteristics that a good father should possess. First, he needs to be the head of the family - **1Co. 11:3**, "But I want you to understand that the head of every man is Christ, the head of a wife is her husband, and the head of Christ is God." Second, one of the most important functions of a father is to protect his children. They should feel and know that they are safe with him. Their whole future is built on that foundation – knowing they can find safety and security in his arms. Third, he needs to provide for them as well as he can. He does not have to earn the rocket scientist's salary, but he must supply the necessities of life and be an example of a good provider.

Showering children with all sorts of worldly things will do little for a healthy regard toward possessions and could teach them to be self-centered and egocentric. Too many men think that gifts are the answer to gaining a child's love when, in fact, they are not. The fourth characteristic of a good father is to discipline his children. **Pro. 13:24** says, "Whoever spares the rod hates his son, but he who loves him is diligent to discipline him." Discipline must be measured to correct errant behavior and not used for self-gratification or empowerment. Done right, it is a primary catalyst for raising a respectable and hard-working child.

Fifth, a good father is a man who shows his children what a loving and faithful husband is. It is critical for his daughter's future to know how to choose a good, honest, and loyal husband and for his sons to witness and emulate a healthy marital relationship. A father's example today will play a massive role in the happiness of his son's and daughter's future marriages. We should use the scriptures as a guide. **Eph. 5:25**, "Husbands, love your wives, as Christ loved the church and gave himself up for her." Faithful husbands also provide a happy household, and happy children are far less likely to become dysfunctional teens and adults.

Finally, while all those characteristics are essential, the one that encompasses them all, and then some, is for him to be a faithful Christian. After all, few who have not committed their lives to the Lord will care about using scripture as a guide for their role as a father. A believer will raise his children scripturally. **Pro. 22:6**, "Train up a child in the way he should go; even when he is old, he will not depart from it." In other words, he will train them to be loyal, respectful, honest, and, above all, faithful to their Savior, and when they are older, they will not give up those beliefs.

The quality of the investment today will determine the quality of their future. Be an example of what you want them to be.

Chapter 89

The Bronze Serpent

"And as Moses lifted up the serpent in the wilderness, so must the Son of Man be lifted up, that whoever believes in him may have eternal life" (**Joh. 3:14-15**). If I were to ask you to recite **Joh. 3:16**, I am convinced you would do so without any hesitation. It is arguably the most "famous" of all the verses in the Bible. But, if I were to ask you what the two verses before that one are, I am equally convinced you might have to look it up. Nicodemus, a respected Pharisee who served in the Jewish high court, the Sanhedrin, came to Jesus at night. Before Nicodemus could even ask a question, which I assume was, "What can I do to inherit eternal life?"

Jesus gave him the answer, "...Truly, truly, I say to you, unless one is born again, he cannot see the kingdom of God" (**Joh. 3:3**). Jesus went on to tell the confused Pharisee that the only way to accomplish that was to be "born of the water and the spirit." (**v. 5**). After further explanation and assurance, Jesus says the words of **Joh. 3:14-15** as a preamble to **v. 16**. Let's begin with some background to the selected verses. Sometime after the beginning of the Exodus, the impatient Israelites question Moses and God with these words, "...Why have you brought us up out of Egypt to die in the wilderness? For there is no food and no water, and we loathe this worthless food." (**Num. 21:5**).

The "worthless" food they loathed was the bread God gave them. How could they have been so unappreciative of God's grace and mercy?

God did not take kindly to their complaining and sent fiery serpents among them. Many of the Israelites were killed by the snakes, and the rest, fearful for their lives, decided to go to Moses and repent of their ungratefulness. Moses prayed for the people, and God said to him in **Num. 21:8**, "Make a fiery serpent and set it on a pole, and everyone who is bitten, when he sees it, shall live." Moses did as the Lord commanded, and any Israelite who was bitten and looked at the bronze serpent was saved.

Similarly, Christ was lifted up on a cross so that we could figuratively "gaze" upon Him and be saved. The weight of our sinful nature is too much for us to bear, and the sting of the sins we commit all leads to our spiritual death.

But looking to the cross where death and evil were once for all defeated by the redemptive blood of Christ is our one chance to be saved. Having then "gazed" upon Christ by realizing his magnificent sacrifice, we are given the opportunity to be saved from those sins.

Knowing that underscores the importance of **Joh. 3:14-16** even more,

"And as Moses lifted up the serpent in the wilderness, so must the Son of Man be lifted up, that whoever believes in him may have eternal life. For God so loved the world, that he gave his only Son, that whoever believes in him should not perish but have eternal life."

Just as the only thing that could save the Israelites was looking at the serpent set on the pole, the only thing that can save us is looking to Jesus Christ on the cross. Without Him, we are lost, doomed to an eternity away from the presence of the Almighty God.

Chapter 90
See Yourself Through His Eyes

"But when Simon Peter saw it, he fell down at Jesus' knees, saying, "Depart from me, for I am a sinful man, O Lord" (**Luk. 5:8**). Simon Peter and his fishing companions had been toiling all night and had not caught a single fish. Upon hearing Jesus' suggestion to put out into deeper waters and drop the nets, the fishermen caught so many fish that the nets started breaking. The astonished Peter then uttered the words of our verse. With a great sense of humility, he vocalized his feelings of unworthiness to be in the presence of the Savior Jesus Christ. Peter was not the only New Testament character to feel that way.

Paul voiced his unworthiness in 1st Corinthians when speaking of the appearance of the Lord after His resurrection. After listing to whom Christ had appeared in person, he speaks the following words in **1Co. 15:8-9**,

> "Last of all, as to one untimely born, he appeared also to me. For I am the least of the apostles, unworthy to be called an apostle because I persecuted the church of God."

Ashamed of his past actions, he could not see himself worthy of the lofty title of apostle, yet look at what God had in store for him.

He would be the man who would take the Good News to the Gentile world and write most of the New Testament books. And men came to that conclusion not only in the New Testament. Throughout the ages, men have spoken similar words when confronted with the power and majesty of God. In **Exo. 3:11**, Moses, chosen to be the liberator of God's people, Israel, deemed himself unworthy of the task at hand with these words, "...Who am I that I should go to Pharaoh and bring the children of Israel out of Egypt?" Men and women feel that way because of man's fallen state.

We can only feel unworthy when we think of the times we doubted Him or were disobedient and sinned. We are sinners, unworthy of the mercy of the Creator, but He does not see us that way. God created us in His image.

Gen. 1:27, "So God created man in his own image, in the image of God he created him; male and female he created them." He did not just slap a few bones together, cover it with flesh, and then leave it half-baked, never realizing its true potential. He made us so perfect that He was pleased when he looked upon His creation. If you were unworthy, would He provide for you? Mat. 6:26, "Look at the birds of the air: they neither sow nor reap nor gather into barns, and yet your heavenly Father feeds them. Are you not of more value than they?"

God values you so much that He was willing to sacrifice His only Son to give you the hope of eternal life in Heaven. But some people are unworthy. Mat. 10:37-38,

"Whoever loves father or mother more than me is not worthy of me, and whoever loves son or daughter more than me is not worthy of me. And whoever does not take his cross and follow me is not worthy of me."

I trust you are not someone who does not love God first and foremost. If you are, God values you much more than you can imagine. Don't see yourself from your perspective; see yourself through His eyes – you will be amazed at what you find.

Chapter 91
The Fallacy of Idolatry

"All who fashion idols are nothing, and the things they delight in do not profit. Their witnesses neither see nor know, that they may be put to shame. Who fashions a god or casts an idol that is profitable for nothing? Behold, all his companions shall be put to shame, and the craftsmen are only human. Let them all assemble, let them stand forth. They shall be terrified; they shall be put to shame together. The ironsmith takes a cutting tool and works it over the coals. He fashions it with hammers and works it with his strong arm. He becomes hungry, and his strength fails; he drinks no water and is faint.

The carpenter stretches a line; he marks it out with a pencil. He shapes it with planes and marks it with a compass. He shapes it into the figure of a man, with the beauty of a man, to dwell in a house. He cuts down cedars, or he chooses a cypress tree or an oak and lets it grow strong among the trees of the forest. He plants a cedar and the rain nourishes it. Then it becomes fuel for a man. He takes a part of it and warms himself; he kindles a fire and bakes bread. Also he makes a god and worships it; he makes it an idol and falls down before it. Half of it he burns in the fire.

Over the half he eats meat; he roasts it and is satisfied. Also he warms himself and says, "Aha, I am warm, I have seen the fire!" And the rest of it he makes into a god, his idol, and falls down to it and worships it. He prays to it and says, "Deliver me, for you are my god!" They know not, nor do they discern, for he has shut their eyes so that they cannot see, and their hearts, so that they cannot understand. No one considers, nor is there knowledge or discernment to say, "Half of it I burned in the fire; I also baked bread on its coals; I roasted meat and have eaten. And shall I make the rest of it an abomination? Shall I fall down before a block of wood?"

He feeds on ashes; a deluded heart has led him astray, and he cannot deliver himself or say, "Is there not a lie in my right hand?" Remember these things, O Jacob, and Israel, for you are my servant; I formed you; you are my servant; O Israel, you will not be forgotten by me" (**Isa. 44:9-21**)

It is easy to look at those verses and pretend they do not apply to us. Most of us do not cut down a tree and use the wood to warm ourselves and make food before taking a piece and carving an idol. We also do not fashion an idol from precious metals and fall down before it. We know that is a ridiculous notion and probably scoff at such "idiotic" ideas, but does that mean we are exempt from practicing idolatry? We may not create them from scratch, but we have our own, and even worse, we take the creations of God and make them our idols.

We make those in His image - actors, singers, sports personalities, models, and political leaders—the objects of our worship. We revere them and take their word as fact without ever investigating their reliability. We fashion ourselves after them and imitate them in a vain attempt to be their likeness. We want to be them. We adore them and live under the illusion that they care about us above the fame and fortune we bring them. When we struggle with the trials of life, we turn to their movies, songs, motivational quotes, and whatever else they spout to help us overcome grief and despair.

We think they can "save" us – and that is the fallacy of idolatry. The temporary relief they give us has dangers attached to it. Our attraction to them draws us like a vile magnet from the arms of God and deposits us into the snares of the evil one. They are of no lasting value to us. They will fade away, and we will have to find a new idol to take their place because they are temporal at best. You are unimportant to them, and they will forget you in time. Hear the words of **v. 21** again, "Remember these things, O Jacob, and Israel, for you are my servant; I formed you; you are my servant; O Israel, you will not be forgotten by me."

Only one God can save you; only one God can mend a scarred human being or a broken heart; only one God loves you so much that He was willing to sacrifice His only son to give you a chance to grasp everlasting life. Only one

God is eternal—**Rev. 1:8**, "I am the Alpha and the Omega," says the Lord God, "who is and who was and who is to come, the Almighty."

Chapter 92

What Does "Church" Mean?

The word "church" is a translation of the Greek term "ecclesia." According to the Theological Dictionary of the New Testament (TDNT), it means "A gathering of citizens called out from their homes into some public place, an assembly"... "an assembly of Christians gathered for worship in a religious meeting," or "the whole body of Christians scattered throughout the earth." The first thing we notice is that there is more than one meaning. The two primary ones are "a gathering of people" and "all Christians." When Jesus said, "I will build my church," it would not have been unfamiliar to the listener, and they would have known what He meant. It is correctly assumed by readers today that the word "ecclesia" used in that context was the larger body of Christ.

The same could be said for **Rom. 12:4-5**,

> "For as in one body we have many members, and the members do not all have the same function, so we, though many, are one body in Christ, and individually members one of another."

Let's look at one more example before continuing. The words of **Col. 3:15** read, "And let the peace of Christ rule in your hearts, to which indeed you were called in one body...". Clearly, then, the words of Jesus and the author of Romans and Colossians are not referring to a physical location but rather the larger body of Christ. Now, opponents will quickly say, "See, it is not a church building," or "We do not need to attend church."

However, there are many instances where a physical location is referred to. We begin with the words of Jesus in **Mat. 18:20**, "For where two or three are gathered together in my name, there am I in the midst of them." Quite obviously, our Savior is referring to a gathering of believers in this instance. We know that numerous specific locations are mentioned in the New Testament. That is evident since we know "ecclesia" means "assembly." We see that in references to the churches in Galatia, Jerusalem, Rome, Ephesus, and various other places, all named for more prominent geographic locations.

Heb. 10:25 refers explicitly to a gathering of believers in a physical location, "...not neglecting to meet together, as is the habit of some..." so the evidence of the scriptures supports us meeting together. "But it never says they met in a church." opponents will say. Sure, New Testament Christians met in the homes of Lydia and Nympha, but remember, there were not readily available buildings for them to meet in, and money was also scarce. Importantly, they did not meet exclusively in homes either.

Act. 2:46, "And day by day, attending the temple together and breaking bread in their homes, they received their food with glad and generous hearts...." Early on, there already was a combination of places they met. I like small churches because of the close bonds they produce, but larger churches can accomplish what smaller ones cannot. God is less concerned with where we meet and more concerned with how we act. Meet at home if you do not like larger churches, but understand that Ecclesia is, by definition, a gathering of Christians, so whether you prefer smaller or larger gatherings, attend church.

Chapter 93
Not Even Jesus Knows

"Now concerning the times and the seasons, brothers, you have no need to have anything written to you. For you yourselves are fully aware that the day of the Lord will come like a thief in the night." (**1Th. 5:1-2**).

Paul, the writer of both 1st and 2 Thessalonians, had just told his audience that they would see their deceased friends again. This assurance was by way of the fact that the living and the dead would be gathered together at the second coming of the Lord. That must have been a relief, but some probably said something like, "Well, Paul, that is comforting, but when will this whole 'second coming' happen?"

They were curious but not the only ones to have asked that question. People have always tried to get a "heads up" on the future, especially concerning the return of Christ. Jesus had to answer more than one question about the future. An example of that is found in **Luk. 21:7** regarding the destruction of the Temple. The disciples asked, "Teacher, when will these things be, and what will be the sign when these things are about to take place?" Jesus did not answer them specifically and only replied that they should not be "terrified" when they heard of wars and tumults because those things did not automatically mean the end.

Over the millennia, various "scholars and prophets" have tried to predict the end time, but no matter how much "inside information" they claim to have or how convincing they appear to be, none of them have been correct. How could that be? They claim to have had revelations or even that they were in the presence of the Lord and were told directly by Him. Let's have the scriptures shed some light on the matter for us. The disciples once again asked Jesus, "Lord, will You at this time restore the kingdom of Israel?" (**Act. 1:6**). Instead of giving them any clue as to the actual date, our Savior has this to say in **Act. 1:7**, "...It is not for you to know times or seasons that the Father has fixed by his own authority."

Jesus wanted them to know that it was not for them to know the will of the Father concerning those things. He told them they would receive the Holy Spirit and be His witnesses in "all Judea and Samaria, and to the end of the earth." Two more interesting verses dealing with this are found in **2Pe. 3:9-10,**

> "The Lord is not slow to fulfill his promise as some count slowness, but is patient toward you, not wishing that any should perish, but that all should reach repentance. But the day of the Lord will come like a thief, and then the heavens will pass away with a roar, and the heavenly bodies will be burned up and dissolved, and the earth and the works that are done on it will be exposed."

I particularly like this reference to the end time because of **v. 9**. God is patient and does not want anyone to perish, but He does not want us to confuse His patience with a personal attitude of "Oh great, I have lots of time." Instead, He wants us to know that the Lord will come suddenly and without warning - as a thief who comes when no one expects it. And notice that there will be no place to hide when He does come. But the very best reason we do not know and why those "end-time prophets" are as wrong as they could be is given to us in the words of Jesus in **Mat. 24:36-39,**

> "But concerning that day and hour no one knows, not even the angels of heaven, nor the Son, but the Father only. For as were the days of Noah, so will be the coming of the Son of Man. For as in those days before the flood they were eating and drinking, marrying, and giving in marriage, until the day when Noah entered the ark, and they were unaware until the flood came and swept them all away, so will be the coming of the Son of Man."

That's right, not even the angels or the Son of Man know when that day or hour will be. Those false prophets are no more knowledgeable about the last day than you and I are, and it is incredibly arrogant to think that they have knowledge even Jesus does not have.

Like the people who were unaware of the coming flood and were caught off-guard by its sudden appearance, so will they be. It is far more profitable for you and me to think of every day as the last day because it may well be. But, something even better than that is to live an obedient life in Christ and do all we are commanded. That way, we will not have to worry about whether the last day is today, tomorrow, or who knows when. And stop listening to deluded souls who think they know something Jesus does not. Live right, and don't worry – it seems the most straightforward and best solution.

Chapter 94

But a Mist

"O Lord, make me know my end and what is the measure of my days; let me know how fleeting I am! Behold, you have made my days a few handbreadths, and my lifetime is as nothing before you. Surely all mankind stands as a mere breath! Selah. Surely a man goes about as a shadow! Surely for nothing, they are in turmoil; man heaps up wealth and does not know who will gather!" (**Psa. 39:4-6**).

The worst mistake anyone can make is thinking that they have more time. When we allow that thought to dominate our minds, we act carelessly, assuming we have enough time to correct our mistakes.

People have often asked me why many churches are made up of predominantly older people. One reason is that as we grow older, we become more aware of our mortality and thus seek answers. That certainly is not the only reason, however. Older, more mature people have a greater understanding of the complexities of life and how incredulous evolution is. Their wisdom draws them to the indubitable truth that God is the creator and sustainer of everything. They embrace the reality of God, put on Christ in baptism, and accept the responsibility and accountability as Christians.

Aside from other reasons, one of the primary ones remains the awareness that life is not "forever," time does not stand still, and is definitely not slow.

By contrast, many younger people think they have an abundance of time left and act in ways contrary to God's commands. They are convinced that sometime in the future, they will be able to step into their Christianity, but for now, they can do as they please. Should we despair and wait for our death every moment of our lives, too scared to live for fear of dying? Of course not. God wants us to share in the beauty of this life, and He wants us to enjoy the adventures that await us, but we need to be mindful of the fleeting nature of life.

Have fun, make plans, and live as if they will happen, but be aware that life is a gift, and tomorrow is not promised. **Jam. 4:13-14**,

"Come now, you who say, "Today or tomorrow we will go into such and such a town and spend a year there and trade and make a profit"— yet you do not know what tomorrow will bring. What is your life? For you are a mist that appears briefly and then vanishes."

Tomorrow is a mystery, and living like it is promised without obedience can lead to an eternity of despair. One hundred twenty people die each minute, which might not seem like that many, but that equates to 7425 each hour and approximately 65 million per year.

Nothing will prevent death from finding us one day, and if we are one of the 7425, today will be our last. That is not meant to be a gloomy, all-is-lost statement but is intended to make you aware of your frailty as a mortal human being. 2Sa. 14:14, "We must all die; we are like water spilled on the ground, which cannot be gathered up again...". Have you ever dropped water on the sand? You cannot retrieve it, and all you see is the witness of how it has influenced the sand for a short while, but before long, it dries, and no more record of it exists. Your influence on Earth is likely going to be like that.

Your loved ones will remember you, and their loved ones may do the same, but your influence on this world will eventually disappear like the water on the sand. Your time and your influence are limited. If you are aware of your fleeting nature and that your time on this earth could end at any moment, you can prepare for a future in Heaven. Why risk the peace and beauty that Heaven has to offer for a lifestyle that promises nothing but fleeting pleasure followed by an eternity of anguish?

Our selfish natures need to put away the things of the world and, instead, put on things of the spirit. Live, love, laugh, embrace the adventure, live like there is no tomorrow, and enjoy the moment, but do so in Christ. Do that, and you will secure for yourself a future that is beautiful beyond your wildest imagination. 1Co. 2:9, "...What no eye has seen, nor ear heard, nor the heart of man imagined, what God has prepared for those who love him". Amen.

Chapter 95
The Seal of Authenticity

We know what the cross meant for Christians. Jesus' flesh symbolized sin and His blood, the new covenant, and our redemption, but we overlook the importance of the resurrection. The cross was the promise of hope, and the resurrection fulfilled that promise. In other words, If Jesus had not risen, He would have been considered a liar or a lunatic, a delusional soul who erroneously thought He was the Son of God. He would have been a mere footnote in history. Because He arose from the grave in such a dramatic fashion, this was the seal of authenticity on everything He was and accomplished.

As the Centurion said on that fateful day when our Savior breathed His last, "Truly, this man is the Son of God!" (**Mar. 15:39**). I can imagine the Devil shouting for joy and thinking how he had won the day, but how he must have anguished when he realized, like everyone else, that the tomb was empty. Satan was defeated once and for all at the resurrection of Christ: **1Co. 15:3-8**,

> "For I delivered to you as of first importance what I also received: that Christ died for our sins in accordance with the Scriptures, that he was buried, that he was raised on the third day in accordance with the Scriptures, and that he appeared to Cephas, then to the twelve. Then he appeared to more than five hundred brothers at one time, most of whom are still alive, though some have fallen asleep. Then he appeared to James, then to all the apostles. Last of all, as to one untimely born, he appeared also to me."

I found the following information in a book by Timothy Keller, "The resurrected Jesus is recorded as appearing in Judea (**Mat. 28:9; Luk. 24:31, 36**) and in Galilee (**Mat. 28:16–20; Joh. 21:1–23**), in town (**Luk. 24:36**) and countryside (**Luk. 24:15**), indoors (**Luk. 24:36**) and outdoors (**Mat. 28:9,16; Luk. 24:15; Joh. 21:1–23**), in the morning (**Joh. 21:1–23**) and the evening (**Luk. 24:29,36; Joh. 20:19**), by prior appointment (**Mat. 28:16**) and without prior appointment (**Mat. 28:9; Luk. 24:15,34,36; Joh. 21:1–23**), close (**Mat. 28:9, 19; Luk. 24:15,36; Joh. 21:9–23**) and distant (**Joh. 21:4–8**), on a hill (**Mat. 28:16**) and by a lake (**Joh. 21:4**), to groups of men (**Joh. 21:2;** **1Co. 15:5,7**) and groups of women (**Mat. 28:9**), to individuals (**Luk. 24:34;** **1Co. 15:5,7–8**) and groups of up to five hundred (**1Co. 15:6**), sitting (**Joh. 21:15** implied), standing (**Joh. 21:4**), walking (**Luk. 24:15; Joh. 21:20–22**), eating (**Luk. 24:43; Joh. 21:15**), and always talking (**Mat. 28:9–10, 18–20;** **Luk. 24:17–30, 36–49; Joh. 20:15-17, 19-29; 21:6-22.**) That is a significant amount of evidence from many people in many places.

Do we, as Christians, need that type of proof? No! Most of us know that Christ is the risen Lord, but it is nice to be able to prove to the nay-sayers that hundreds of people evidenced his brief return to earth before his ascension. One more quick point. Have you ever wondered why the most critical two events, the death of Christ on the cross and His resurrection, are only commemorated every couple of months by some and even less by others? And why is communion on the Lord's Day celebrated so infrequently despite verses like **Act. 20:7**, "On the first day of the week, when we were gathered together to break bread..."? Because people don't study the Bible and accept its teachings as the truth.

It's funny how the same groups who think it is unimportant to take communion weekly do not apply the same "whenever you feel like it" to the offering.

Chapter 96
Peace After Justification

"Therefore, since we have been justified by faith, we have peace with God through our Lord Jesus Christ. Through him we have also obtained access by faith into this grace in which we stand, and we rejoice in hope of the glory of God. Not only that, but we rejoice in our sufferings, knowing that suffering produces endurance, and endurance produces character, and character produces hope, and hope does not put us to shame, because God's love has been poured into our hearts through the Holy Spirit who has been given to us" (**Rom. 5:1-5**).

Many Christians are familiar with **Rom. 5:3-5**, but far fewer are familiar with **v. 1-2**. The first three words of **v. 3** suggest that it is a continuation of the preceding two verses, so today, we will look closely at "we have peace with God." Paul is speaking to Christians and basically says, "Christ was the atonement for the sins of everyone, thereby becoming the propitiation and ensuring the believer's redemption to be justified as righteous and be sanctified." Those who have been previously justified find themselves at peace with God, but were we not at peace with Him before that?

Jam. 4:4 states,

"You adulterous people! Do you not know that friendship with the world is enmity with God? Therefore, whoever wishes to be a friend of the world makes himself an enemy of God."

Obviously, we were not. We are never truly at peace with our enemies. Even a truce is there for the breaking, and any period of peace will be uneasy at best. We are a fallen people who, by nature, war against God. The Devil loves that and will use whatever he can to further the conflict. In his mission to separate us from the love of God, war works in his favor.

When we finally decide to put Christ on in baptism and are justified, we enter into a peace accord with the sovereign God. Peace was also the gift Jesus left not only to His disciples but to us, as well. **Joh 14:27**, "Peace I leave with you; my peace I give to you. Not as the world gives do I give to you. Let not your hearts be troubled, neither let them be afraid." Moreover, when we are no longer at war, we no longer need to be afraid, and life becomes stress-free and easy. Unfortunately, there is a widespread belief nowadays that God is a God of peace, incapable of wrath, and would never wage war against humanity.

That belief falsely frees mankind from accountability for their actions since there is no consequence for any behavior. But that is simply not the case. He is a just God and will punish the unjust accordingly. He is not weak-minded and does not allow us to get away with sin just because of His love for us. It is an uncomfortable truth, for sure, but God hates sin and will not tolerate sinners,

> "For you are not a God who delights in wickedness, evil may not dwell with you. The boastful shall not stand before your eyes; you hate all evildoers." (**Psa. 5:4-5**).

If we are not justified before Him, we are at war with the creator of heaven and earth. And that is not a good situation to be in because there is no way to win, period. Understand where you are with God, and then, if need be, take the proper steps to ensure that you are at peace with Him. Just remember that it is God who offered us peace first by offering up His Son so that we may stand before Him a new creature.

Chapter 97
If only...

"...and to grant relief to you who are afflicted as well as to us, when the Lord Jesus is revealed from heaven with his mighty angels in flaming fire, inflicting vengeance on those who do not know God and on those who do not obey the gospel of our Lord Jesus. They will suffer the punishment of eternal destruction, away from the presence of the Lord and from the glory of his might" (**2Th. 1:7-9**).

People who do not believe in God have little concern for an afterlife. Their refusal to hear and accept the word of God leaves them in a precarious position, though, even if they deny that reality.

Denying something does not negate its existence, no matter how firm that belief is. It is easy for them to say He does not exist, but when the Day of Judgment comes, they will be found wanting and only have the "punishment of eternal destruction" to look forward to. They choose not to believe not because of a lack of evidence for the existence of the Creator, but because of the lack of foresight. They choose to lead a sinful life. Ignorance is bliss and rules the day. I wish they would take the time to understand the danger of what awaits them if they are wrong. It is also doubtful that they really understand what "forever" or "eternity" means.

As mortal, linear human beings, we cannot understand that time will ever have no end. If we could, we would be much more inclined to ensure we are on the right side of eternity. We basically have three possible destinies as humans. First, if no God exists, we will die and then simply cease to exist. If that were the case, forever would have no consequence. Much of the world subscribes to this philosophy. Unfortunately for this first group, not believing in God does not make Him any less real or the consequences of unbelief any less devastating. The second and third options are closely connected because they are religious in nature. Faithful, obedient believers will find themselves in Heaven forever, whereas unrepentant sinners will find themselves in Hell forever.

Deny God if you like, but the Day of Judgment will come, and you will be rewarded for what you did on earth. **Mat. 13:47-50,**

> "Again, the kingdom of heaven is like a net that was thrown into the sea and gathered fish of every kind. When it was full, men drew it ashore and sat down and sorted the good into containers but threw away the bad. So it will be at the end of the age. The angels will come out and separate the evil from the righteous and throw them into the fiery furnace. In that place, there will be weeping and gnashing of teeth <forever>."

No matter how strong your denial is, there will come a day when you will be forced to face the reality of God. **Rom. 14:11,** "For it is written, "As I live, says the Lord, every knee shall bow to me, and every tongue shall confess to God." If only they would look at the evidence; if only they would understand their choice has eternal consequences; and if only they would make the right choice.

Chapter 98
A Tough Decision to Make

"Do not think that I have come to bring peace to the earth. I have not come to bring peace, but a sword. For I have come to set a man against his father, and a daughter against her mother, and a daughter-in-law against her mother-in-law. And a person's enemies will be those of his own household.

Whoever loves father or mother more than me is not worthy of me, and whoever loves son or daughter more than me is not worthy of me. And whoever does not take his cross and follow me is not worthy of me. Whoever finds his life will lose it, and whoever loses his life for my sake will find it. 'Whoever receives you receives me, and whoever receives me receives him who sent me'" (**Mat.10:34-40**).

Have you got a family member or friend who belittles your Christianity? Do they make fun of you or insult you because you believe in "utter nonsense"? Maybe even a spouse cannot accept your devotion to Christ. My wife and children are all devoted believers, but I have family members who are disparaging toward me because of my choice to be a believer. Conversations must be carefully navigated because any "slip" could lead to angry rebuttals. There are also the constant innuendos and insults to deal with. While we desire to see every one of our family members in Heaven one day, we sadly must accept the reality that some will not be there by their own choice.

It does not prevent us from speaking to them, but we also need to understand that, ultimately, the decision is theirs to make. Another reality must be faced. What do you do when a loved one is so against your religious beliefs that the relationship becomes toxic? What if that relationship causes you to stumble in your Christian faith? How do you balance your need to be accepted by family and friends with your desire to be Christ's true and faithful servant? Often, the unwillingness to be at odds with the former means we step out of our Christianity to save the relationship.

Sometimes, we try to please both our earthly friends and our spiritual Father, but that is a precarious tightrope to walk. It could result in us being at odds with the scriptures and the real danger of foregoing the promise of an eternity in Heaven. I am not advocating that you throw away your family and friends and live the life of a secluded monk, but be aware of where your spiritual enemies may be lurking. Sometimes, the thing you love most on this earth is the most dangerous thing to your Christianity. What if that relationship causes you to stumble in your Christian faith?

Yes, you could have an uneasy peace where you subdue your Christian enthusiasm. You could always walk on eggshells to avoid offending the other person's sensitivities. It is a dangerous path, but you could choose it. But, if that relationship will cost you your salvation, there is another path you may have to consider – cut the anchor that will drown you spiritually. By saying if we love a parent more, we are not worthy of Him. Christ emphasizes that there should be nothing hindering our relationship with Him.

Don't just give up; go to the person and try to come to an understanding, but if they are still unable to accept your Christianity, it may be time to make a tough decision. Choose this day whom you will serve – "...but as for me and my household, we will serve the Lord" (**Jos. 24:15**).

Chapter 99
Put the Sledgehammer Away

"Have nothing to do with foolish, ignorant controversies; you know that they breed quarrels. And the Lord's servant must not be quarrelsome but kind to everyone, able to teach, patiently enduring evil, correcting his opponents with gentleness. God may perhaps grant them repentance leading to a knowledge of the truth, and they may come to their senses and escape from the snare of the devil, after being captured by him to do his will" (**2Ti. 2:23-26**).

This is the third time in this paragraph that Paul advises Timothy not to engage in pointless controversies (**vs. 14, 16**).

People like to win, there is no doubt about that, and social media has given everybody with an opinion an opportunity to state it as an indisputable fact to secure victory. The truth matters little as no corroborating evidence is introduced to support a position – victory is the only thing that matters. Total annihilation of the "idiot" opposing their views leads to pages and pages of disputes, quarrels, slander, and rage. The worst is that I refer to the multitudes of verbal fights that occur almost daily between Christians in real life, especially on social media sites like Facebook.

Paul was not referring to Christians quarreling with other Christians, but the sad fact is that if we cannot even respect each other, how would we respect those who oppose our Christianity? And how would they respect us? In respect to the context, do you become embroiled in endless quarrels with those who oppose your Christian views? I will be the first to admit that I have been guilty of that in the past. We cannot fathom their ignorance, so we become angry and resort to beating them with the Bible to slap some sense into them. And then, because our pride gets ahead of our common sense, we refuse to extricate ourselves from the quarrel and escalate the conflict further.

Paul does not want us to act that way. "...the Lord's servant...", which means you and me, should not be quarrelsome, "but kind to everyone." We need to learn how to discuss our differences, not as the world does, using fear and rage, but with the gentleness of Christ. When we speak, we should do so with the patience of a "nursing mother taking care of her own children" (**1 Th. 2:7**). Kindness goes a long way, and we should never forget that we project Christianity with our actions. We do not speak for ourselves when we approach or react to those who are still in the world.

When we speak, we speak for Him, "Therefore, we are ambassadors for Christ, God making his appeal through us..." (**2 Co. 5:20**). That's right, brothers and sisters, we are His ambassadors. God uses us to deliver His message to seeking ears, even if they do not appear to be so initially. We have all heard of the saying, "Think before you speak," and nothing is truer, whether we are dealing with fellow Christians or unbelievers. Our actions determine the destiny of those we speak to, so we should choose our words carefully and act in the most loving way possible. Also, remember that the world is watching when you fight with other believers. Stop trying to win an argument with a figurative sledgehammer, or better still, don't needlessly quarrel in the first place.

Chapter 100

Don't Judge a Sinner While Committing the Same Sin

"Though they know God's righteous decree that those who practice such things deserve to die, they not only do them but give approval to those who practice them" (**Rom. 1:32**).

Paul has just listed sins, including covetousness, malice, envy, murder, strife, deceit, gossip, slandering, boasting, and those disobedient to their parents. He then sternly warns the Roman church to be careful not to approve of those who "do such things," especially if they do the exact same. In **Rom. 2:1-2**, he continues the thought with the following,

"Therefore you have no excuse, O man, every one of you who judges. For in passing judgment on another you condemn yourself, because you, the judge, practice the very same things. We know that the judgment of God rightly falls on those who practice such things."

When someone commits the same sins they judge others for committing, they condemn themselves. Almost every day, a Christian brother or sister seems to fiercely judge others in the church for doing something they are doing. A perfect example of this is gossip. The individual approaches someone and "discusses" a third party's faults. Desperate for an ally, they circle their wagons by throwing the "guilty" person under the bus. They spend as long as they have a listening ear in gossip about the tendency the object of their judgment has to gossip. It gets even more complicated, however.

Even as we listen to them and realize they are doing the same, we often allow them to continue for some unfathomable reason. In doing so, we condone the sin of gossip and become active participants, complicit in the same. We are told to admonish those who sin in **Gal 6:1-2,**

"Brothers, if anyone is caught in any transgression, you who are spiritual should restore him in a spirit of gentleness. Keep watch on yourself, lest you too be tempted."

Notice how we are warned not to be tempted to do the same. In **1Co. 15:33**, we read the following, "Do not be deceived: "Bad company ruins good morals.""

When we listen to gossip, say nothing to someone cheating on a spouse, or remain silent even as we know someone has committed theft or some other sin, our good morals are ruined. We are so desperate to keep a friendship intact that we are willing to forego doing what we know is right. We excuse our behavior by saying that the other person deserves it or that no harm was intended, but nothing good will come from it. Instead of participating in their sins, we should correct them for the sake of their salvation. But we must also do so with the right intentions and spirit.

To admonish is to "express warning or disapproval in a gentle, earnest or solicitous manner" or "to give friendly earnest advice or encouragement to." That is why Paul says in **Gal.6:1** to do so in a "spirit of gentleness." A true friend will not hesitate to call out another for their wrongdoings, but their approach will be one of caring concern. No one reacts to harsh, accusatory words, but most will listen to an admonishment, especially when it comes from a place of genuine Christian concern. But be careful not to do so in a judgmental manner as Paul so eloquently puts it in **Rom. 2:3**, "Do you suppose, O man – you who judge those who practice such things and yet do them yourself – that you will escape the judgment of God?" Don't proclaim judgment on sinners while committing the same sin – it will not end well for you.

Don't miss out!

Visit the website below and you can sign up to receive emails whenever John "Cleve" Stafford publishes a new book. There's no charge and no obligation.

https://books2read.com/r/B-A-HYTDB-WFSWC

BOOKS 2 READ

Connecting independent readers to independent writers.

www.ingramcontent.com/pod-product-compliance
Lightning Source LLC
Chambersburg PA
CBHW032117040426
42449CB00005B/174